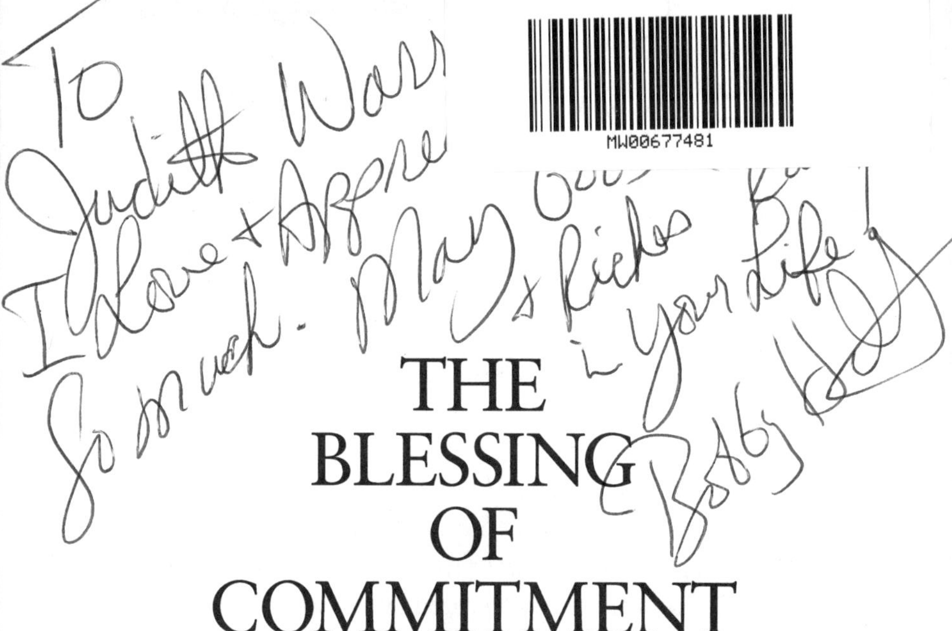

THE BLESSING OF COMMITMENT

Releasing Wealth and Riches into Your Life

 Unless otherwise indicated, all Scripture quotations are taken from the *King James Version* of the Bible. Verses marked Amplified are Scripture taken from *The Amplified Bible*. Emphasis within Scripture is the author's own.

ISBN 1-930766-25-4

For Worldwide Distribution
Printed in the USA

Bishop Bobby Hilton Ministries, Inc.
690 Northland Blvd.
Forest Park, OH 45240
(513) 851-WORD (9673) • Fax: (513) 742-3458
Web-site: www.bobbyhilton.org
E-mail: info@bobbyhilton.org

Cover Design by RIGHTSYDE GRAPHICS, INC.

This book is dedicated to all of the following with sincere appreciation...

I first express praise, worship, adoration, and appreciation to my **Lord and Savoir Jesus Christ** for selecting me for such a time as this to take His Word to the World. I am honored to be a servant to the body of Christ, helping to bring clarity and understanding to our heritage as declared by the Word of God.

The Lord blessed me with such a wonderful helper, suitable to assist with the call on my life. My wife and soul mate of twenty-three years, **Lady Valda Hilton.** I love you so much! Thank you for being there with me through all the seasons of our lives.

Ministry requires many hours away from family. I'm not sure people really understand the sacrifice families endure while leaders are doing the work of the Lord. I thank my son **Jermaine** and daughter **Stephanie** for understanding and sharing me with so many others. I love you both very much!

I'm so thankful that the Lord allowed my parents **Bishop Lewis Hilton, Sr.** and **Mother Sarah Hilton** to be in good health and see how marvelously He is blessing the ministry. You've been praying for me all of my life. Thank you for your prayers and never ending support. I also want to thank **Mother Dorothy Bostick**, my spiritual mother. I very much appreciate your prayers and support.

To my sisters, **Martha Dillingham, Bertha Southall, Joyce Thomas, Angela Hilton**, my brother **Chris Hilton,** and all of your respective spouses; thanks for supporting me over the years. God has been real good to us!

It's simply amazing how the Lord will send the right people into your life just at the right time. This happens when we are doing something that will ultimately glorify Him. **June Ridgway Daniels,** you are truly an on time blessing from the Lord. Thank you for your endurance with this project. You were determined to see it through and you did. I also appreciate **Josie Wilson** and **John Dawkins** for assisting you with the many hours it took to bring this to fruition. We will always cherish the memories of our dear **Tamico Green** who worked on this project for a short period of time before her life on this earth was concluded. We'll rejoice with her in heaven.

Karen Hite, Angie Vega, Kimberly Lee, and **Ann McGhee,** what can I say. You all have proven your love for the ministry and me many times. Your steadfast assistance with this and all the many projects of the ministry will never be forgotten.

Anthony Hunter and **Timothy McClure,** you both are great and represent just a sampling of the wonderful staff members who do their best to assist me in the work of the ministry. I cannot express how thankful I am that God brought the two of you into my life. Thanks to all of **my staff personnel** for being there for me.

The Church Family of Word of Deliverance Ministries for the World, Inc. is one of the greatest congregations in the World. I am so thankful the Lord allowed me the honor of being the pastor of such a beautiful body of believers. Thank you all so much for your prayers.

Bishop Bobby Hilton Ministries, Inc. Covenant Partners, what a joy it is to my soul to know that the Lord would impress upon the hearts of people all over the world to assist with what He has given me to do. I thank you partners for your prayers and support.

I must give a special thanks to the long list of men and women of ministry who have sown into my life including the late **Bishop John W. Barber, Bishop T.D. Jakes, Dr. Creflo Dollar, Pastor Rod Parsley, Bishop Carlton Pearson, Bishop Eddie Long, Joyce Meyer, Evangelist Shirley Caesar, Evangelist Dorothy Norwood** and so many others too numerous to name.

God bless you all!

"To God Be the Glory"

TABLE OF CONTENTS

Preface ix

Introduction xiii

Chapter One—It's Time for a Change 1

Chapter Two—Can You Stand To Be Blessed? 19

Chapter Three—Total Deliverance 27

Chapter Four—Much More Than Enough 37

Chapter Five—Determined To Praise 45

Chapter Six—Get in Position 55

Chapter Seven—The Word in Us 67

Chapter Eight—Spiritual Commitment 87

Chapter Nine—Spiritual Adultery 101

Chapter Ten—The Lust Factor 121

Chapter Eleven—The Battle is the Lord's 131

Chapter Twelve—Run with Patience 145

Chapter Thirteen—Commit to a Holy Life 159

Chapter Fourteen—He Loves You 169

PREFACE

The Bible is very clear about the blessing God has declared in the heavenlies for His people who are committed to Him. It is God's desire to release the blessing and when we place ourselves in a position of obedience, He will make sure we obtain it. In the appointed time everywhere we go, everything we have, and everything we do shall be blessed!

Throughout the history of mankind, God has sent forth the message of *the blessing of commitment* to His people to strengthen, encourage, and remind us that He loves us and is faithful to His Word. After the death of Moses, the Lord spoke to Joshua about the *blessing*. He told Joshua that He had given him every place the sole of his feet tread upon and assured him that no man would be able to stand before him all the days of his life. The Lord let Joshua know that He would be with him just as He had been with Moses (see Joshua 1:1–7). Joshua 1:8 says:

> *This book of the law shall not depart*
> *out of thy mouth; but thou shalt*
> *meditate therein day and night,*
> *that thou mayest* ***observe to do according***
> ***to all that is written therein:*** *for then*
> *thou shalt make thy way* ***prosperous,***
> *and then thou shalt have* ***good success.***

Job was strengthened and encouraged after hearing a word on *the blessing of commitment*. Elihu, one of Job's friends who had been listening to him lament about his devastating misfortunes, told Job that if God's people obey and serve Him, they shall spend their days in prosperity, and their years in pleasures (Job 36:11).

God used the prophet Malachi to remind His people of the *blessing* He has declared for those who follow His instructions and obey His commandments. Malachi 3:10 says:

Bring ye all the tithes into the storehouse,
that there be meat in mine house,
and prove me now herewith, saith the Lord
of hosts, if I will not open you the windows
of heaven, and pour you out a blessing,
that there shall not be room enough to receive.

Moving forward in time to the New Testament, the writer of Hebrews delivered a message to God's people about *the blessing of commitment*. Hebrews 10:35-36 in *The Amplified Bible* reads:

Do not, therefore, fling away
your fearless confidence, for it carries
a great and glorious compensation of reward.

For you have need of steadfast patience
and endurance, so that you may perform
and fully accomplish the will of God,
and thus receive and carry away
[and enjoy to the full] what is promised.

The church at Corinth was also strengthened and encouraged when reminded of *the blessing of commitment*. Paul wrote:

But as it is written, Eye hath not seen,
nor ear heard, neither have entered into
the heart of man, the things which God
has prepared for them that love him.
(1 Cor. 2:9)

Like the prophets of old, my purpose for presenting this book to the body of Christ is to be obedient to the call of God, and once again deliver His eternal message of blessing to His people who are committed to Him. God's Word never changes—it is the same yesterday, today, and forever. The psalmist wrote:

Commit thy way unto the Lord;
trust also in him, and he shall bring it to pass.
(Ps. 37:5)

Great is God's faithfulness! He will do what He said He would do. He will command the blessing (Deut. 28:8), therefore be confident that you will prosper and have good success. I know you will not be disappointed because He promised to never fail nor forsake us. Continue to study His Word, worship and praise Him, then you shall receive *the blessing of commitment. Wealth and riches* shall be released into your life. He's a Mighty God—the King of Glory, Prince of Peace, and The Lord Our Savior. He's Our Strong Tower, Sure Foundation, and Our Everlasting Father. Let us give God honor and glory as we endeavor to live totally committed to Him.

Bishop Bobby Hilton

INTRODUCTION

We are living in a divine time on the clock of Heaven. God has determined that during this moment in history His glory shall be revealed through His people. This is a time of manifestation where the world will look at us and see the blessings and favor God bestows upon those who are committed to Him. A glorious outpouring of God's Spirit is coming to the body of Christ proving to the world that He is God and holds all power in His hand.

We are blessed to be alive in these days—God is moving mightily on behalf of His people. This is the season our ancestors longed for. Many who lived before us were slaves, immigrants, and laborers suffering with barely enough to make ends meet. Yet they held fast to their faith in God and His Word as they continued to pray, trusting that future generations would experience the fulfillment of God's promises. Hebrews 11:13 tells us:

These all died in faith, not having received
the promises, but having seen them afar off,
and were persuaded of them,
and embraced them, and confessed that
they were strangers and pilgrims on the earth.

God sets appointed times for His will and purpose to unfold and come forth. He always has a plan to deliver His people and bring them to a wealthy place (Ps. 66:12). The Lord never intended for people who are "in the world" to be more prosperous than His children—He wants us to be blessed. When we commit to Him and follow His instructions, wealth and riches shall be in our homes (Ps. 112:1–3).

To those accustomed to traditional doctrine regarding prosperity, the message I present in this book may seem radical. People who operate with a mentality of scarcity might have difficulty believing that this Word is for them. Many Christians are taught that money is the root of all evil and these same Christians believe they are supposed to have enough to just get by in order to remain humble. Please realize, the Bible says that the *love* of money is the root of all evil (1 Tim. 6:10).

Now is the time for the body of Christ to rise. God's favor is upon us, but our minds must be open to believe and receive it. We must no longer accept the spirit of lack; it is not of God. The Word says He came that we might have life and have it more abundantly (John 10:10).

The Lord gives us power to get wealth (Deut. 8:18) and when He blesses us it is for His glory and purpose. Christians must be liberated from the mind-set of "not enough" and "just enough." We serve the God of *much more than enough* (El Shaddai).

Of course, the enemy is not going to let us grab hold of this message without opposition. Salvation is a gift, but we must fight for our inheritance. The Bible tells us: "...the kingdom of heaven suffereth violence, and the violent take it by force" (Matt. 11:12b). We must be prepared to *take* what belongs to us.

The concept that Christians are supposed to be wealthy and rich at first glance might appear extreme to some, but as you will see it is all the Word of God. Position yourself to receive everything God has declared for you. You can receive *the blessing of commitment*. God will *release wealth and riches into your life*—His Word declares it. Get ready to experience the manifestation of God's glory in this divine time on the clock of Heaven.

ONE

IT'S TIME FOR A CHANGE

God has given me a word on *The Blessing of Commitment* and placed it deep inside my spirit. This word is not just for one individual, church, or denomination; it is for the entire body of Christ. God is ready to do some fantastic things for us. A *releasing* is coming. Deliverance is coming. But it is going to require our commitment.

The enemy has many of God's people in a place where we accept the things he is doing to us. It's time to declare war on the devil! This is a new millennium and a change is coming to the house of God!

The Bible backs up this message—God's Word is in front of it and surrounds it. Let's begin with one of the foundational Scriptures from the Word of God concerning *the blessing of commitment*. Romans 12:1 says:

I BESEECH you therefore, brethren, by the mercies of God, that ye present your bodies a living sacrifice, holy, acceptable unto God, which is your reasonable service.

To receive this blessing there must first be a commitment to God, His Word, and a lifestyle that pleases Him. I am going to show you by the Word of God that once you make this commitment, you will not be second place in anything. Romans 12:2 says:

And be not conformed to this world: but be ye transformed by the renewing of your mind, that ye may prove what is that good, and acceptable, and perfect, will of God.

Transformed in this verse means a change in our way of thinking. *The Amplified Bible* says it this way:

Do not be conformed to this world (this age), [fashioned after and adapted to its external, superficial customs], but be transformed (changed) by the [entire] renewal of your mind [by its new ideals and its new attitude], so that you may prove [for yourselves] what is the good and acceptable and perfect will of God, even the thing which is good and acceptable and perfect [in His sight for you].

You can receive *the blessing of commitment*, but you must be transformed. It's time for a "mind change!"

THE SPIRIT OF DEBT

A yoke of bondage captivates many Christians. This spirit from the enemy must be rebuked, cursed, and cast out. I am talking about the spirit of debt. This spirit comes to destroy individuals, marriages, and families. It literally drives people out of their minds. It is a curse from the devil and it's time for the saints to be delivered.

It is not God's will for His people to be in debt. God wants us delivered from debt. Wealth and riches are in God's Kingdom and it is time for the saints to possess them. But we must have a commitment to God. We cannot accept one part of the Word and reject the other. We must do that which is pleasing to Him, and His will shall come forth in our lives.

Unfortunately, for many Christians, debt has become a custom and a way of life. It has been accepted as a part of living on earth. For example, the world encourages us to get as many Visa and MasterCards as we can. We're told to get charge cards at Sears, JC Penney's, and of course Saks Fifth Avenue, then charge them to the limit!

Many of you are paying on charge accounts and don't know what is being paid for. Your bills have been over a $1,000 for so long you can't remember what you bought. People are wearing mortgaged shirts, mortgaged suits; your shoes and socks are mortgaged. You purchase your underwear on a charge card at 21 percent interest and you don't even own your shorts! Someone else owns everything you have. Something is wrong with that and it's time for a change.

You write a check for $90 to Visa, $65 for the other Visa, $75 for MasterCard, $15 to Sears, and $28 to JC Penney's. You have to pay a house note and car note, utilities, and telephone bills. You get to the house of God, the offering is called and you say, "I don't have any more money." *I guess not!*

Remember ye not the former things,
neither consider the things of old.
(Isa. 43:18)

It's time to stop the old way of doing things. Anyone who doesn't have discipline with credit cards should cut them up. Some people can get a credit card in the mail on Tuesday afternoon and by that same night it's up to the limit. Here's a common scenario: you get that credit card, call a friend and say, "Let's go shopping. The Lord blessed me with a Visa!" You head for the mall and before you know it, the Visa is charged to its limit. The next month the same friend calls you back, asking if you are going shopping. Your response is, "I can't. Pray for me, I need prayer. The devil has me bound!"

Some of you might say, "It's too late for me" or "I'm in too much debt." It is not too late. Deliverance is coming to the people of God and I am going to show you by His Word that it's our time now. The glory of God is going to shine throughout the earth. It is time for the saints to get what belongs to us, but we must have a transformed mind. A change must take place in our minds. We need to realize what God has for us and what He will do if we take hold of His Word.

NO MORE PART-TIME SAINTS

You must understand, it doesn't matter where you are, what's happening in your life, or how long its been going on. I am going to give you the Word and this Word is going to deliver you. God is moving. This message is for those who are committed to God, live a faithful life, and walk in righteousness and truth. God is tired of part-time believers. This message is not to the part-time saints, but to those who are giving God their all and fully committed.

I have to "open your mind" so you can receive all that God has for you. You are included in His will and testament. It doesn't matter how low you've been; it's time to come out! One thing was wrong with the children of Israel; when they came out of Egypt they still had a slave mentality. The children of Israel had been down so long that they had no idea how to come up. God had blessed them and given them a land. He had given them everything they needed, but their minds were not able to receive it.

IT'S NOT TOO HARD FOR GOD

Is any thing too hard for the LORD?
At the time appointed I will return unto thee,
according to the time of life,
and Sarah shall have a son.
(Gen. 18:14)

Abraham was asked, "Is anything too hard for the Lord?" It doesn't matter how much debt you are in; it's not too hard for God. *The blessing of commitment* is not about you—it's about God. The Lord is going to bring you out of debt to show Himself to the world.

Everyone may not be able to receive this word. Some people might say, "I don't want any money, I just want to be free. All I want is peace." I am telling you there is no peace without money. The Bible lets us know, "...but money answereth all things" (Eccles. 10:19b).

A BLESSING AND A CURSE

People incorrectly quote Scripture saying, "Money is the root of all evil." They don't want to have money because they believe money is the root of all evil. The Bible does not say that. It says, "For the love of money is the root of all evil" (1 Tim. 6:10a). This means those who will do the wrong thing to get money will find themselves in a mess. You don't have to sell drugs to get money, nor do you have to cheat or hoodwink anyone. Scams and shams won't get you God's blessing.

Behold, I set before you this day
a blessing and a curse;
(Deut. 11:26)

Some of you may feel troubled when you read this. You tell yourself, *but Bishop Hilton said "I don't have to be broke, busted, and disgusted."* You have to know that the Word says you can be blessed, therefore I say you can be blessed. The Lord sets before you a blessing and a curse. The choice is yours.

A blessing, if ye obey the commandments
of the LORD your God,
which I command you this day:

And a curse, if ye will not obey the
commandments of the Lord your God...
(Deut. 11:27–28)

You may wonder what the above Scripture is referring to when it says "a blessing." It means you are empowered to prosper, equipped to succeed, and positioned to live in abundance. How does one receive this blessing? Obey the commandments of the Lord our God. You must follow God's instructions and be totally committed. Whatever you say you are going to do, do it with all your heart.

GOD WANTS US BLESSED

I want everyone to understand that it is God's will for His people to live in prosperity. Look at Deuteronomy, chapter 28. Note how it describes the blessing God has promised to those who are committed to Him:

AND it shall come to pass,
if thou shalt hearken diligently
unto the voice of the LORD thy God,
to observe and to do all his commandments
which I command thee this day, that the
LORD thy God will ***set thee on high***
above all nations of the earth:

And all these blessings shall come on thee,
and overtake thee, if thou shalt hearken
unto the voice of the LORD thy God.

Blessed shalt thou be in the city,
and blessed shalt thou be in the field.

Blessed shall be the fruit of thy body,
and the fruit of thy ground,
and the fruit of thy cattle,
the increase of thy kine,
and the flocks of thy sheep.

Blessed shall be thy basket and thy store.

Blessed shalt thou be when thou comest in,
and blessed shalt thou be when thou goest out.

The LORD shall cause thine enemies that rise
up against thee to be smitten before thy face:
they shall come out against thee one way,
and flee before thee seven ways.

The LORD shall ***command the blessing***
upon thee in thy storehouses,
and in all that thou settest thine hand unto;
and he shall bless thee in the land
which the LORD thy God giveth thee.

The LORD shall ***establish thee an holy***
people *unto himself, as he hath*
sworn unto thee, if thou shalt ***keep the***
commandments *of the LORD thy God,*
and walk in his ways.

And all the people of the earth shall see that thou art called by the name of the LORD; and they shall be afraid of thee.

And the LORD shall ***make thee plenteous in goods****, in the fruit of thy body, and in the fruit of thy cattle, and in the fruit of thy ground, in the land which the LORD sware unto thy fathers to give thee.*

The LORD shall ***open unto thee his good treasure****, the heaven to give the rain unto thy land in his season, and to* ***bless all the work of thine hand:*** *and thou shalt* ***lend*** *unto many nations, and thou shalt* ***not borrow.***

And the LORD shall ***make thee the head,*** *and* ***not the tail;*** *and thou shalt* ***be above only,*** *and thou shalt* ***not be beneath;*** *if that thou* ***hearken unto the commandments of the LORD thy God,*** *which I command thee this day, to observe and do them:* *(Deut. 1–13)*

The Lord will set us *high* above all nations. He will command the blessing on us. He will establish us as *holy people* unto Him—if we *keep His commandments* and *walk in His ways*. God will bless us with *plenty* of everything we need and open His *good treasure* to us. All of our work will be blessed, and we will *lend* and not borrow. He'll make us the head and not the tail, *above* only and not beneath. *The blessing of commitment* is for the saints who *hearken diligently* unto the voice of the Lord and do all His commandments.

Many have thought it was a sin to be "too blessed." How can the people of God be too blessed? We should know that a change is coming into our lives and the set time for this blessing is now. This is not just a confession; it's a manifestation!

Let's not have any misunderstanding; there is a time to confess the Word. But once we make a confession, we must start walking by faith with praise and thanksgiving. We must believe that God is going to do what He says and that His Kingdom shall come forth. This is not about us, but about the glory of God being revealed through us. When the saints are blessed, we are blessed so the world may see God through the blessing.

Please let me caution you. Walking by faith does not mean we just wait on God to take care of us. Faith without works is dead (James 2:26). Paul wrote about this in his letter to the saints in Thessalonica:

...that if any would not work,
neither should he eat.
(2 Thess. 3:10b)

It is not a welfare mentality that comes from God; God declares wealth and riches for His people. Welfare may be needed for a season in your life. You might find yourself in a predicament, but if you are young and healthy you don't have any business *staying* on welfare.

GENERATION TO GENERATION

Our ability to acquire wealth is often hindered because of bad habits that are passed down from generation to generation. For example, the first thing young people want to do when they come of age is get credit. They believe they are adults when they have a credit card in their name. Next, they accumulate debt. Then they accumulate too much debt. God has given me a word to decree against the spirit of debt. We do not have to be in bondage to debt anymore. Many parents have the audacity to pass this debt mentality on to their children. Their children see them suffering in debt as they hear the bill collectors calling. Unfortunately, these children grow up thinking this is an acceptable lifestyle.

Many parents focus on Proverbs 22:6 for instruction and encouragement in teaching their children. This Scripture says:

Train up a child in the way he should go:
and when he is old, he will not depart from it.

This verse is often repeated in the church. Everyone reads Proverbs 22:6, but why don't people read the next verse, which says:

The rich ruleth over the poor,
and the borrower is servant to the lender.

Proverbs 22:7 must be taught also! God is not calling us to be enslaved to anyone but Him. In other words, it's time to provide our children with sound financial advice. If something cannot be paid for in thirty days, don't buy it. Most of us have to finance our cars and our homes, but God is bringing us out of that mind-set as well.

It's time to stop paying almost $300,000 for a house that sold for $100,000. Let me show you what I mean. The monthly payment for a $100,000 mortgage financed for thirty years at 8.5 percent interest is $768.92. If we add all the monthly payments ($768.92 x 360 months), we see that the house really costs $276,809. That's $176,809 in interest! A better plan is to pay one-half of the monthly payment ($384.46) every two weeks. By doing this, you are actually making one extra mortgage payment ($768.92) each year. You can then add an extra amount of money, for example $25, to each payment. The total amount paid out is now $201,976 and the mortgage is paid off in nineteen years instead of thirty, and you save $74,833!

We need to realize we can own the house we live in free and clear. The world system tells us that we are supposed to have a mortgage our entire life. However, the Word of God tells us to owe no man anything (Rom. 13:8).

Many people have so much debt they don't know where to start. You can begin by taking your smallest debt, pay it off first, and then work your way up to the largest debt. Avoid credit card pre-approval letters that you receive in the mail; they can be snares from the devil.

God does not want you to live in debt, He wants you to be an overcomer and help free someone else. He wants you to be able to support the Kingdom. Remember, the Word of God says in Romans 12:2, "And be not conformed to this world: but be ye transformed by the renewing of your mind." God is not only going to give us houses and cars; He is going to let us pay them off. He's releasing us from the bondage of debt. Are you ready to be blessed this way?

A TRANSFER OF WEALTH

God wants the body of Christ to go in a new direction and move in a new way. Proverbs 13:22 reads:

A good man leaveth an inheritance
to his children's children: and the wealth
of the sinner is laid up for the just.

In *The Amplified Bible* this Scripture reads:

A good man leaves an inheritance
[of moral stability and goodness]
to his children's children,
and the wealth of the sinner
[finds it's way eventually]
into the hands of the righteous,
for whom it was laid up for.

As you can see in the above Scripture, the Word of God declares that the wealth and riches of the sinner is ours. That's why we should not fret nor feel envious when it appears as if the sinner man is prospering in his ways (Ps. 37:1,7). We can say, "This is good. Do the best you can with it because soon it will be ours." A transfer of wealth and riches is coming to the body of Christ—out of the hands of the sinner into the hands of the saints.

We are destroyed because of the lack of knowledge (Hos. 4:6). It's time to gain a better understanding of God's Word regarding wealth and riches. The devil has been holding up our finances long enough. People come to church week after week depressed because of debt. We have to be released from the spirit of debt. We are coming out and going forward. We'll have a new way of thinking and a new way of living. When God sees us in proper position and in expectation, we will walk ourselves into a blessing. *The blessing of commitment* will be commanded upon us.

God is so faithful. We had two young men visiting our church one Sunday morning who had been travelling extensively. They told me that they had been hearing this message on commitment preached across the nation. God has blessed them for their commitment. While in California, they walked right into a $32 million blessing. It all started when they shared the Word of God with a man who was Catholic. This man got saved, filled with the Holy Ghost, and started speaking in other tongues. Through this newly spirit-filled gentleman, they signed a contract with a company that is involved in movie productions and television commercials. Now that's what I call a transfer of wealth!

I have been told not to minister this message because there are still many people not living in obedience to the Word of God. Some think I should only teach about living right. I will always teach about living right. However, the enemy will try to get us to believe that we cannot go forward until everyone lives right. But the Lord showed me if we individually obey His commandments, He will individually bless us. Our neighbors can act like fools as long as they want to. They don't have to live holy. They can covet, lie, steal, and cheat. They can do whatever they choose, but I choose to obey God's commandments and be blessed.

IT'S IN THE HOUSE

Many of us question if the Lord really delivers people from debt. 2 Kings 4:1–7 shows us there is an anointing that delivers us from debt.

Verse 1:

NOW there cried a certain woman
of the wives of the sons of the prophets
unto Elisha, saying, Thy servant
my husband is dead; and thou knowest
that thy servant did fear the LORD:
and the creditor is come to take
unto him my two sons to be bondmen.

This woman's husband left her in so much debt that the creditors came and asked her how she was going to pay them. All the woman had of value was her two sons.

Verse 2a:

And Elisha said unto her,
What shall I do for thee?
tell me, what hast thou in the house?

What this verse is telling us is to stop looking for answers to come from a distance; it's in the house. Elisha asked the woman what she had in her house. Often what we need for our deliverance is already in the house!

Verse 2b:

And she said, Thine handmaid hath not
any thing in the house, save a pot of oil.

Verses 3–6:

Then he said, Go, borrow thee vessels
abroad of all thy neighbors,
even empty vessels; borrow not a few.

And when thou art come in, thou shalt
shut the door upon thee and upon thy sons,
and shalt pour out into all those vessels,
and thou shalt set aside that which is full.

So she went from him, and shut the door
upon her and upon her sons, who brought
the vessels to her; and she poured out.

And it came to pass, when the vessels
were full, that she said unto her son,
Bring me yet a vessel. And he said unto her,
there is not a vessel more. And the oil stayed.

God Almighty (El-Shaddai: The God of More Than Enough) gave this woman a miracle from the oil and the vessels that were in her house. We must start with what we have.

Verse 7:

Then she came and told the man of God.
And he said, Go, sell the oil, and pay thy debt,
and live thou and thy children of the rest.

Elisha told the woman to pay her debt and live. The Lord came that we might have life and that we might have it more abundantly (John 10:10).

THE LORD WILL MAKE US RICH

Many of us have made mistakes financially. You may have spent money you did not have and gotten yourself into debt, but you do not have to continue living like this. You do not have to live in a debt-ridden house. God's Word declares that *wealth and riches* shall be in your house (Ps. 112:3).

The blessing of the LORD, it maketh rich,
and he addeth no sorrow with it.
(Prov. 10:22)

Most Christians understand that the will of God is to heal our bodies and save our loved ones. But the Word of God also tells us that the Lord will make us rich! I didn't say it! The Word of God says it! Let's get ready to receive the blessings of the Lord.

THE ANOINTING DESTROYS THE YOKE

And it shall come to pass in that day,
that his burden shall be taken away
from off thy shoulder, and his yoke
from off thy neck, and the yoke shall be
destroyed because of the anointing.
(Isa. 10:27)

This foundational Scripture tells us that the blessings of the Lord are going to expand upon us fully. Because of the anointing, the burden of debt that has had so many "yoked up" for so long, will be destroyed.

Can your mind receive this word from God on *the blessing of commitment*? Are you ready for a *releasing of wealth and riches into your life*? Ask yourself these questions:

- Am I committed to God, His Word, and a lifestyle that pleases Him?
- Have I allowed the Glory of God to flow through my life?
- Have I received the Word of God that will cancel debt out of my life?
- Have I received the Word of God that says He makes me rich?

PRAYER OF REPENTANCE

Father, in the precious Name of Jesus, I magnify Your holy Name. Lord, help me position myself to be used in Your Kingdom. Let Your glory shine through my life. Forgive me for my foolish ways. I repent for spending money I did not have and getting myself into debt. I now ask You to transform my mind. I am going to walk by Your Word. I will live by Your Word. I am coming out of debt. I will no longer be beneath. I shall be above. I will no longer be the tail. I shall be the head. I will no longer allow the spirit of debt to hold me in bondage. I shall live in prosperity. I press into You. I stand upon Your Word. I present my body as a living sacrifice, holy, and acceptable to You. I totally submit to Your Word. I receive Your promise that wealth and riches shall be in my house. Help me to allow You to make me rich, that I may support the Kingdom. In Jesus' Name. Amen.

TWO

CAN YOU STAND TO BE BLESSED?

The God we serve is "all-powerful" (omnipotent) and "all-knowing" (omniscient). He is present everywhere (omnipresent). When we press into Him, we do not have to be bound by anything. God is real and He continues to work miracles in the lives of His people.

God is looking for people who are properly positioned, those who guide themselves to a place of obedience, respecting Him for who He is. Isaiah 1:19 says:

If ye be willing and
obedient, ye shall eat
the good of the land.

The Word of God tells us that the riches of the land are ours, but we must be in right relationship with Him to receive manifestation. Let's study this further.

Having the right mindset; stay humble, treat others right

As they were increased,
so they sinned against me:
therefore will I change
their glory into shame.
(Hos. 4:7)

This verse in the *The Amplified Bible* reads:

The more they increased and multiplied
[in prosperity and power],
the more they sinned against Me;
I will change their glory into shame.

God increased His people in prosperity and power, but they did not know what to do with it. This is where we get the question, *"Can you stand to be blessed?"*

Some people are afraid to have money because they cannot handle it. In other words, they allow money to rule them. In the time of Hosea, the people sinned against God when He blessed them. Unfortunately, this continues to happen today. For instance, if the Lord blessed some people with wealth and riches, they would buy a big boat. Instead of being in church on Sunday mornings, they would be on their boats.

We should not serve other gods when we increase in prosperity. This is a sin against God. God is going to rain down *the blessing of commitment and release wealth and riches*, but it is going to be on the saints who know what to do with it!

WE SHALL PROSPER

And they rose early in the morning,
and went forth into the wilderness of Tekoa:
and as they went forth, Jehoshaphat stood
and said, Hear me, O Judah, and ye
inhabitants of Jerusalem; Believe in the
LORD your God, so shall ye be established;
believe his prophets, so shall ye prosper.
(2 Chron. 20:20)

When you believe the Word of God and obey His commandments, you will prosper. The spirit of debt should not be in your home. God's Word declares that you shall have success. The world system does not want you to receive this kind of teaching because you become dangerous to the enemy with this knowledge. The enemy does not want you to know about the anointing that releases the yoke of debt. But God told me, "This yoke is coming off My people."

CAN GOD TRUST YOU TO GIVE ACCORDING TO HIS WORD?

God has a purpose for blessing those who are committed to Him. He prospers us to finance His Kingdom. When God finds trustworthy people, He blesses them even more. Leviticus 27:30 tells us:

And all the tithe of the land, whether of the
seed of the land, or of the fruit of the tree,
is the LORD's: it is holy unto the LORD.

This Scripture is difficult for some people. The Word of God says the tithe is the Lord's and it is holy unto Him. God must be able to trust you with the tithe. You cannot say, "God when You send that $60,000 to me, then I'll give my tithe." If you only have $6.00 give Him 60¢! You shouldn't bluff the Lord by saying what you would do if you had more money. A lot of people who gamble make all kinds of promises to God. *Lord, if you let me hit the Powerball, I'll buy the things the church needs. In fact, I'll pay off the church's mortgage!* How can God trust you to pay the tithe on $200 million when you aren't paying it on $32,000? (Please note that I am not saying that it is okay to play the lottery as long as you pay tithes on the winnings!)

You must be faithful with what you have. He isn't going to trust you with a large amount of money if you won't do what's right with a small amount. If you find an excuse with a little money, you'll find an excuse with a lot. *Well God, I was going to tithe but I've got to pay for something else first—I'll be back.* This attitude won't work with Him!

God is generous when it comes to His instructions concerning tithing. He requires only 10 percent of your gross income. Have you looked at your paycheck deductions lately? The government takes out more than that!

I've heard people say, "I'm not giving 10 percent to the church! The Pastor must think I'm crazy. I need a new car. Does he really think I'm going to give $25 a week and drive an old car?" Let me share something with you. I used to be the church van driver because I did not have a car, but I still gave God what belonged to Him—tithes.

THE LORD'S PENALTY AND LATE FEE

God also has instructions for those who borrow from the tithe. Leviticus 27:31 says:

> *And if a man will at all redeem ought of his tithes, he shall add thereto the fifth part thereof.*

Let's do the math. The tithe is 10 percent. Therefore, the tithe for $100 is $10. If you keep or borrow from it, according to Leviticus 27:31, you are to add the fifth part. The fifth part is 20 percent. Twenty percent of $100 is $20. This means when you keep that $10 today, planning to pay it back to the Lord next week, you need to calculate what you really owe. You owe $10 plus the fifth part, that is $20, for a total of $30. Some of you may be having heart palpitations! I want you to understand that the Lord has a penalty and late fee.

The prophet Malachi warns us about the consequences of not paying our tithes. Malachi 3:8–9 says:

> *Will a man rob God? Yet ye have robbed me.*
> *But ye say, Wherein have we robbed thee?*
> *In tithes and offerings.*
>
> *Ye are cursed with a curse: for ye*
> *have robbed me, even this whole nation.*

Blessings come when we learn and carry out the Word of God. Curses come to those who oppose and defy it. If we want to receive *the blessing of commitment* we must be determined to do what's right. We must adhere to His Word in our lifestyle and in our giving.

Blessings are a testimony of God's goodness. For example, if you are living in a nice house it isn't just for you to say, "Look at my nice house." You should say, "Look at what the Lord has done for me." The reason we have anything is because of God. He blesses us with health, shelter, protection, food, and clothing. We must be faithful in giving to God. The more we give, the more we will receive. He will rain blessings on us because it is the Father's good pleasure to give us the Kingdom (Luke 12:32).

GOD REWARDS OBEDIENCE

We have a member of our congregation who has always been faithful with her tithes and offerings. She was a nurse for a home health agency. One evening she went to visit a client she had previously worked for through the agency. She prayed for this gentleman, anointed him with oil, and spent some time talking with him.

The man told her, "I'm so glad you came. I haven't felt this good in a long time." He took out his checkbook and gave her a check for $4,000. He told her that he wanted her to come and work for him. By the time she left the man's house she had $5,000. He had given her an advance on her first paycheck!

She came to the church to show me the check and to share with me that she had been praying about becoming self-employed. This member did not want to work for an agency; she believed God had a greater plan for her life. She had also been praying about giving the church a special offering of $1,000. Today, this member does not work for an agency. She has her own agency and she was able to bless the ministry. God prospered her for being obedient.

Offer unto God thanksgiving;
and pay thy vows unto the most High:
And call upon me in the day of trouble:
I will deliver thee,
and thou shalt glorify me.
(Ps. 50:14–15)

When you are faithful in doing what God has commanded you to do, you can call upon Him. He promises to deliver you, but you must offer thanks unto Him and give your tithes.

Save now, I beseech thee, O LORD:
O LORD, I beseech thee,
send now prosperity.
(Ps. 118:25)

The Lord is releasing prosperity now! Increase is coming to God's people and He will be glorified. *We can stand to be blessed.*

THREE

TOTAL DELIVERANCE

While I was ministering *the blessing of commitment* to my congregation, many people gave testimonies of their deliverance. A woman who had been attending these services came to the church on a Friday before leaving for vacation in St. Thomas, Virgin Islands. She told me, "I never felt anything like this in my life. I've been delivered from smoking. I haven't wanted a cigarette and I haven't had any withdrawal symptoms. I'm free in Jesus' Name."

This woman had smoked cigarettes for over twenty years. She didn't have to use a patch. She didn't need a 21-day plan. All she needed was the power of the Name of Jesus. She said, "I have to be a part of this ministry" and joined our congregation that day.

Let me take a moment to explain what being *delivered* means. To be delivered means to be made free from bondage or strongholds of addictions or any entanglements of sin.

Jesus Christ delivers and makes free those who receive Him, allowing the Holy Spirit to dwell and empower their lives. People who have been delivered have been made free from the things that have held them in bondage. Thank you Jesus!

No one has to leave the church the way they came. We should not be embarrassed; all of us have been delivered from something. During this teaching I encouraged individuals at Word of Deliverance to bring their cigarettes, beer, alcohol or any other substance that had them bound. I wanted the people to lay them all on the altar. Everyone was instructed to write intangible strongholds on a piece of paper and place it in my hand. The altar was filled with cigarettes, bottles of alcohol, marijuana, and pieces of paper. We praised God for destroying these tools the enemy uses to keep people in bondage.

Some wanted to stay "behind the scenes." However, many others came to the altar during church services. They didn't wait until church was over, they didn't ask me for a private meeting, and they didn't care who saw them. They came boldly to the altar to be delivered. When we confess that we have a problem and reach the point where we are tired of it, God will break all chains. Let God have His way. Whom the Son has made free, is free indeed (John 8:36)!

STRONGHOLDS WILL COME DOWN

The Word of God says in 2 Corinthians 10:4, "For the weapons of our warfare are not carnal." In other words, this war is not won with our flesh or natural abilities. "But mighty through God," His power, Spirit, and anointing, "to the pulling down of strongholds."

The power of God was present to destroy every stronghold of the devil. I asked the people to confess the things that were holding them in bondage. I told them to speak to that spirit and tell it to loose them in the Name of Jesus. I laid hands on and prayed for many people in the congregation. Every addiction of the devil had to go! The saints will not be in bondage to anything: *total deliverance* is part of *the blessing of commitment*. Praise God!

After several weeks of an outpouring of God's delivering power, we gathered everything that had been placed on the altar. Just as the anointing fire of the Holy Ghost destroys the yoke of the devil, we burned each item. This symbolized the devil's destruction and the freedom of God's people.

Some may wonder why I would have people bring these tools of bondage to the altar. I serve a God who chooses things the world calls foolish to confound the wise (1 Cor. 1:27). God wants a delivered body of believers, people who have a testimony of who He is. As our deliverer, fire baptizer, Holy Ghost-filler, and sanctifier, He never changes. He is the same yesterday, today, and forever (Heb. 13:8).

SEEK GOD FIRST

God is calling the church to a higher level. Fellowship with our Lord should not occur just one day a week. Many people who are struggling with strongholds need to learn how to have fellowship with the Savior everyday. When we're in the presence of the Lord, the devil cannot be there too. Psalm 55:17 says:

Evening, and morning, and at noon,
will I pray, and cry aloud:
and he shall hear my voice.

We must set aside time everyday to be with Him. Getting up two minutes before its time to get into the shower will not work. We have to be determined to seek God first and as we show Him our commitment, He will bless us.

PULLING DOWN THE STRONGHOLD OF DEBT

All of us need an expectation of deliverance. We should also know that the Lord can do it for us. In 2 Kings, chapter 6, we see where God miraculously delivered someone out of debt.

Verses 4–5:

So he went with them. And when they came
to Jordan, they cut down wood.
But as one was felling a beam,
the ax head fell into the water: and he cried,
and said, Alas, master! For it was borrowed.

This poor man cried out to Elisha when he dropped the ax head into the water. He had borrowed this ax head. Consequently, he was in debt and he was in trouble. We all know it is usually not a big problem if you accidentally put a little dent on your own car. However, it is another situation when you let someone use your car and that individual puts a scratch on it.

Verse 6:

And the man of God said, Where fell it?
And he shewed him the place.
And he cut down a stick,
and cast it in thither;
and the iron did swim.

Iron does not float! This man was given a miracle because he was doing the work of God. Therefore, God was not going to allow him to remain in debt.

Verse 7:

Therefore said he, Take it up to thee.
And he put out his hand, and took it.

Whatever it takes, God will bring us out—if we believe in Him. Regardless of what is happening in your life, you can receive *total deliverance.* Raise your expectations concerning the blessings of God. Expect the anointing of the Holy Ghost to destroy every yoke of bondage. Expect your loved ones to be healed and delivered! Credit reports can miraculously come up clean! He is preparing us for this time. The blessings of God are being released and His people are rising.

People sometimes say, "What difference does it make? I'm going to die in debt." You don't have to die in debt, but if you do you have died in bondage. God is coming for a people He's made free.

Everything God does for us is for His glory. He will deliver us to give Himself glory. The God we serve will give us wealth and riches so that He may be glorified. When we are blessed, His glory is revealed.

BLESSED TO BE A BLESSING

And I will make of thee a great nation,
and I will bless thee, and make thy name
great; and thou shalt be a blessing:

And I will bless them that bless thee,
and curse him that curseth thee:
and in thee shall all families
of the earth be blessed.
(Gen. 12:2–3)

God is speaking to Abram (God later renames him Abraham) in this verse. God told Abram He was going to bless him and make his name great. He also told Abram that he would be blessed to be a blessing.

When God gave Abram this word, Abram did not have many material possessions. We know from the Scriptures that his wife Sarai was "a fair woman to look upon." In today's terminology, Sarai was beautiful. Before they went down to Egypt, Abram, fearing that the Egyptians would kill him to take her, told his wife:

Say, I pray thee, thou art my sister:
that it may be well with me for thy sake;
and my soul shall live because of thee.

And it came to pass, that when Abram was
come into Egypt, the Egyptians beheld
the woman that she was very fair.

The princes also of Pharaoh saw her,
and commended her before Pharaoh: and
the woman was taken into Pharaoh's house.

And he entreated Abram well for her sake;
and he had sheep, and oxen, and he asses,
and menservants, and maidservants,
and she asses, and camels.

And the LORD plagued Pharaoh
and his house with great plagues
because of Sarai Abram's wife.

And Pharaoh called Abram, and said,
What is this that thou has done unto me?
why didst thou not tell me
that she was thy wife?

Why saidst thou, She is my sister? so I might
have taken her to me to wife: now therefore
behold thy wife, take her, and go thy way.

And Pharaoh commanded his men
concerning him: and they sent him away,
and his wife, and all that he had.
(Gen 12: 13–20)

Just as Abram feared, when Pharaoh saw Sarai he took her into his house and gave Abram many riches because he wanted Sarai. But the Lord allowed great plagues to enter

Pharaoh's house because she was someone else's wife. After Pharaoh found out that Sarai was married to Abram, he told Abram to take Sarai and leave.

And Abram was very rich in cattle,
in silver, and in gold.
(Gen. 13:2)

Abram left Egypt wealthy. He had all the oxen, camels, sheep, donkeys and servants Pharoah had given him and his riches multiplied.

GET YOUR STUFF!

Know ye therefore that they which are of faith, the same are the children of Abraham.

And the scripture, foreseeing that God would justify the heathen through faith, preached before the gospel unto Abraham, saying, In thee shall all nations be blessed.

So then they which be of faith are blessed with faithful Abraham.
(Gal. 3:7–9)

The same blessings that were promised to Abraham are promised to us through faith in Jesus Christ. We are the people of faith and since Abraham was blessed, we should be blessed too. We must get our "stuff" because we cannot bless anyone unless we are blessed.

HEIRS ACCORDING TO THE PROMISE

Christ hath redeemed us from the curse of the law, being made a curse for us; for it is written, cursed is everyone that hangeth on a tree:

That the blessing of Abraham might come on the Gentiles through Jesus Christ; that we might receive the promise of the Spirit through faith.
(Gal. 3:13–14)

And if ye be Christ's, then are ye Abraham's seed, and heirs according to the promise.
(Gal. 3:29)

Now we, brethren, as Isaac was, are the children of promise.
(Gal. 4:28)

Jesus died on the cross to bring the blessing of Abraham to the Gentiles. We are heirs according to the promise. This promise is to all of Abraham's seed. If you belong to Christ then you are Abraham's seed.

Many of us can testify that the Lord has delivered us from the bondage of debt. In this new millennium, the testimony of the entire body of Christ should be, "We're free! We have no debts!" When a need arises in the church, we'll be able to write the check!

A woman called me one day and said she and her husband had asked God to forgive them for getting into debt. They had already gone to a lawyer to file bankruptcy. The lawyer had not filed the papers because they didn't have all of the money to pay him. Their lawyer called them later and told them he was going to return the money they had given him. He advised them to use that money to pay their sole remaining bill. The Lord had canceled the rest of their debt. Within two weeks after hearing this Word, God gave them a miracle. He has miracles for us. He's ready to prosper and lift us up!

But seek ye first the kingdom of God,
and his righteousness; and all these
things shall be added unto you.
(Matt. 6:33)

It is the Father's good pleasure to bless us, but we must first be committed to Him. We must be faithful and serve Him. When we seek God first, we can receive *total deliverance.*

FOUR

MUCH MORE THAN ENOUGH

God is good and He is a wonderful Savior. We serve a mighty God. If the Lord had not been on our side, where would we be? We must be thankful to God for all He is and for what He is doing in our lives.

Learning about *the blessing of commitment* helps us to understand more about God and His power. The Word of God says, "but the people that do know their God shall be strong, and do exploits" (Dan. 11:32b). Exploits are exceedingly mighty things. Those who believe in His name and put their trust in Him will do exceedingly mighty and great things.

And they spake unto Moses, saying,
The people bring much more than enough
for the service of the work,
which the LORD commanded to make.
(Ex. 36:5)

We declare this passage of Scripture in every service at Word of Deliverance before we receive an offering. This is a powerful statement. In this verse the people were bringing much more than enough. The question is "Where did the people get much more than enough?" At the beginning of the book of Exodus, the children of Israel did not have anything. They were in bondage. They had been in slavery for more than 400 years. Where did this wealth come from? Let's start at Exodus, chapter 3, and learn how God planned not only to set His people free, but also give them wealth.

YE SHALL NOT GO EMPTY

And I will give this people favour in the sight of the Egyptians: and it shall come to pass, that, when ye go, ye shall not go empty:

But every woman shall borrow of her neighbour, and of her that sojourneth in her house, jewels of silver, and jewels of gold, and raiment: and ye shall put them upon your sons, and upon your daughters; and ye shall spoil the Egyptians.

(Ex. 3:21–22)

God is telling His people that when He frees them from the Egyptians, they are not going to leave empty-handed. Likewise, when we get saved, we are not going to be saved and left empty. When we get delivered, we're not going to be delivered and left empty. The wealth of the wicked belongs to the saints. God is just setting it up so that we get what is already declared ours. God never meant for the wicked to keep the wealth. He made everything that is glorious and valuable for His people. The wealth of the wicked is laid up for the just (Prov. 13:22).

Speak now in the ears of the people,
and let every man **borrow** *of his neighbour,*
and every woman of her neighbour,
jewels of silver, and jewels of gold.
(Ex. 11:2)

The use of the word *borrow* makes it appear as though the Egyptians are lending these things to the children of Israel. The Egyptians surely did not intend for the children of Israel to keep these valuables.

And the LORD gave the people favour
in the sight of the Egyptians, so that they lent
unto them such things as they required.
And they spoiled the Egyptians.
(Ex. 12:36)

And Moses said unto the people, Fear ye not,
stand still, and see the salvation of the
LORD, which he will show to you to day:
for the Egyptians whom ye have seen to day,
ye shall see them again no more for ever.
(Ex. 14:13)

God would not allow the Egyptians to hold His people in bondage any longer. He will deliver us as well, but we must open our minds and allow Him to do it. God is telling us, "No more bondage!"

Thus the LORD saved Israel that day out of the hand of the Egyptians; and Israel saw the Egyptians dead upon the sea shore.
(Ex. 14:30)

Now we see how the people were able to bring *much more than enough* for the service of the work, which the Lord commanded to make. If the children of Israel saw the Egyptians dead upon the seashore, they must be out of debt. Even though what they had was borrowed, the couldn't repay the dead Egyptians! They came out of Egypt loaded with silver, gold, and everything else they needed. God put the money and the riches in the hands of the children of Israel. *Wealth and riches* were released into their lives.

For some of you, it looks like you're so low and so far behind financially, you can't see yourself *coming out.* But if God did it before, He'll do it again! We must arm and position ourselves to be in a place where God can use us for His purpose and glory. He's going to bless us so we can live in prosperity while serving Him.

IT'S FOR THE KINGDOM

Take ye from among you an offering unto the LORD: whosoever is of a willing heart, let him bring it, an offering of the LORD; gold, and silver, and brass
(Ex. 35:5)

After giving His people wealth, the Lord asked them to bring an offering. God placed the wealth in their hands so they would bring it into His Kingdom.

And they came, every one whose heart stirred him up, and every one whom his spirit made willing, and they brought the LORD'S offering to the work of the tabernacle of the congregation, and for all his service, and for the holy garments.
(Ex. 35:21)

And they received of Moses all the offering, which the children of Israel had brought for the work of the service of the sanctuary, to make it withal. And they brought yet unto him free offerings every morning.
(Ex. 36:3)

God transferred the wealth. The Egyptians were stripped of their possessions for the benefit of the Kingdom. God *releases wealth and riches* upon His people when we are committed to Him.

GOD'S PRINCIPLE OF INCREASE

Let's turn our attention to 2 Corinthians, chapter 9. Here the apostle Paul explains God's principle of increase. When we operate in the principles of God, we can expect an increase. In other words, our harvest will come.

Verse 6:

But this I say, He which soweth sparingly shall reap also sparingly; and he which soweth bountifully shall reap also bountifully.

Those who sow seed sparingly into the Kingdom of God will reap sparingly. Whoever sows generously will reap generously. Sowing seed into the Kingdom of God refers to the giving of our money, time, skills, gifts, and talents. God supplies the seed; therefore everything we possess is for His glory. As we sow generously into the Kingdom of God, He will rain more blessings down on us.

Verse 11:

Being enriched in every thing
to all bountifulness, which causeth
through us thanksgiving to God.

We're being made rich in every way so that we can give generously for the glory of God. God is ready to bless us so abundantly that any need within the body of Christ will be met.

God does not mind us being rich. As a matter of fact, He wants us to live in prosperity (see 3 John 1:2). Something is wrong when the world can build the most fabulous structures, drive the most fabulous cars, and live in the most fabulous homes—while the saints are barely making it. That's a lie from the pit of hell. Unfortunately, the enemy has many church leaders afraid to teach this message of prosperity.

SEED + GOOD GROUND + WATER + TIME = HARVEST

Some people say, "I gave last week and I haven't seen anything. I gave $56.75, and I needed my increase this week and didn't get it." We all should know that when a seed is planted in the ground it takes some time to get a harvest. But the harvest is coming.

I have never been a farmer and never had a garden. Even though I have not personally done these things, I understand and have seen that once a seed is planted, if you come back the next day you would not see a crop! It takes time for those vegetables to grow. The important thing is to put your seed into good ground. Once you know the ground is good and you water your seeds sufficiently, you'll get the harvest.

Be not deceived; God is not mocked:
for whatsoever a man soweth,
that shall he also reap.
(Gal. 6:7)

Sowing your seed in good ground plus watering it with your praise equals harvest. Don't get weary in your well doing, for in due season you will reap the blessing if you faint not (Gal. 6:9). You can expect a harvest, but you can't reap what you haven't sown.

God has wonderful plans for His people, but we must be committed to His Word. God gives seed to the sower. If He sees us being a sower, He will give us more seed to sow (1 Cor. 9:10). The manifestation of every promise of God's Word will come forth in our lives. It's all for His glory. God is canceling debt and going to cancel even more debt so that we can tell the world "God did it!" We'll be blessed with *much more than enough*.

FIVE

DETERMINED TO PRAISE

Many people are *searching*. Some people are alcoholics because they are *searching*. Others are drug addicts because they are *searching*. Some are even addicted to sex because they are *searching*...

We will never experience fulfillment in our innermost being until we are in proper relationship with God. We were created to worship Him and until we fulfill our purpose for which we were created, we will continue to search. In the book of Isaiah, chapter 43, the Bible says:

Even every one that is called
by my name: for I have created him
for my glory, I have formed him;
yea, I have made him.

This people have I formed for myself;
they will shew forth my praise.
(Isa. 7, 21)

When we praise Him, we show forth His praise. It is through people who are *determined to praise* that the world will see the glory of God.

SHOW THE WORLD WHO JESUS IS

The world is searching for the way, the truth, and the life. It is looking for people who know who Jesus is. Christians should not be depressed or hopeless like nonbelievers. This doesn't mean we won't go through difficult times. But when we go through our difficulties, we go through them dancing and praising God. We have a testimony. We're not stuck—we're coming out!

Everything we do should honor the Lord. When we go to our jobs, we should go honoring the Lord. It's a shame when Christians in the workplace have their lips stuck out further than the people who aren't saved.

The world is watching us. We say we're different. We say we're saved. Yet, too many believers use profanity just as fast as nonbelievers. Every day our lives should show a difference. Many people cannot imagine this Jesus we are talking about. They must see our transformed lives. They're looking at our actions and reactions. When Christians honor the Lord at all times, it's a rebuke to the enemy. It messes the devil up!

It's easy to conduct yourself in a manner that glorifies God when everything is going well. You have plenty of money in your pocket. Everyone is saying good things about you. You have a good job. You can shop at the mall. Your check is coming on Friday. You have plenty of food in the cabinets. It's easy to say, "Bless God!" The house note is paid, car note is paid, and you are feeling good. You're ready to shout, "What a mighty God we serve!"

However, there will be times when you will need the Word of God hidden deep in your heart. The Bible lets us know that sometimes God allows the devil to come after us. In the book of Job, chapter 1, God asked the devil, "Have you considered my servant Job?" The Lord knew Job had been worshipping Him. Job was perfect, upright, and strong. The devil tried to convince God that Job was righteous because everything in his life was going well. But God was confident Job would stay faithful to Him regardless of the circumstances (see Job 1:1–12).

PASS THE TEST

Why did God allow the devil to "test" Job? He allowed it because there is no testimony without a test. When we were in school, we attended class. However, we did not pass the class until we passed the test. Too many people sitting in church won't take the test and pass it. *Passing the test* takes us to a higher level in Christ.

Teachers can sometimes look at their students and know if they are paying attention. However, the real proof of what was learned comes when it's time for the exam. We might as well accept that when exam time comes for the saints, we have to pass. Our commitment to God is going to be tested.

We can't go to the next level until we pass that test. When we operate by the Word of God, we can pass the test.

The blessing of commitment: releasing wealth and riches into your life is a powerful word. The devil is not going to sit back and let us be comfortable. When given the opportunity, he's going to come and test us to see if we'll keep dancing and praising the Lord. When everything is going wrong, stand on the Word of God that says, "But my God shall supply all your need according to His riches in glory by Christ Jesus" (Phil. 4:19).

We haven't danced until we've danced in the furnace. Real praise is praising God in troubled times and dark times. When the Lord blesses us, some of us have a little cute dance. But when hell is all around us, it's time to grit our teeth, put a serious look on our faces, and dance on the devil's head. God inhabits the praises of His people (Ps. 22:3). We must keep lifting the praises up!

WE'RE COMMANDED TO PRAISE HIM

PRAISE ye the LORD. *Blessed is the man that feareth the LORD, that delighteth greatly in his commandments.*

His seed shall be mighty upon earth: the generation of the upright shall be blessed.

Wealth and riches *shall be in his house: and his righteousness endureth for ever.*

Unto the upright there ariseth light
in the darkness: he is gracious,
and full of compassion, and righteous.

A good man sheweth favour,
and lendeth: he will guide
his affairs with discretion.

Surely he shall not be moved for ever:
the righteous shall be
in everlasting remembrance.

He shall not be afraid of evil tidings:
his heart is fixed, trusting in the LORD.

His heart is established, he shall not
be afraid, until he see his desire
upon his enemies.

He hath dispersed, he hath given
to the poor; his righteousness endureth
for ever; his horn shall be
exalted with honour.

The wicked shall see it, and be grieved;
he shall gnash with his teeth, and melt away:
the desire of the wicked shall perish.
(Ps. 112)

We are commanded to praise the Lord. We cannot follow His instructions grudgingly. The Word of God says the blessing is released to those who delight in His commandments. Wealth and riches shall be in our homes.

LET YOUR PRAISE BE HEARD AT ALL TIMES

O bless our God, ye people,
and make the voice
of his praise to be heard:
(Ps. 66:8)

It is so important to bless the Lord at all times. We must bless Him regardless of what we have or don't have. We must bless Him when people like us and when they don't. We need to tell Him how good He's been to us. We should let Him know we appreciate what He has done for us. Let's just bless the Lord!

Some people complain that our praise is too loud at Word of Deliverance. But God's Word instructs us to praise Him so it can be heard. We're not murmuring or groaning, nor are we complaining. We're not waiting until we get a good report. Instead, we're praising Him right now. We're praising God before we see the manifestation of the blessing and making sure that our praises are heard "on high."

Luke 12:32 tells us:

Fear not, little flock; for it is
your Father's good pleasure to
give you the kingdom.

God wants to give us the Kingdom. We can praise Him despite adversities because He strengthens us to go through. He gives us the ability to praise Him in the midst of trouble and provides what we need to have victory.

PRAISE GOD BECAUSE OF HIS WORD

For thou, O God, hast proved us:
thou hast tried us, as silver is tried.

Though broughtest us into the net;
thou laidst affliction upon our loins.

Thou has caused men to ride
over our heads, we went through fire
and through water: but thou broughtest
us out into a wealthy place.
(Ps. 66:10-12)

Some believers would stay at home or sit in church with their heads down in this scenario. The psalmist describes afflictions upon our loins, men riding over our heads, and going through fire and water! At this point many are having sleepless nights and popping pills to relieve their stress. They don't know where to go or what to do. Yet, even during these times we must be determined to praise Him knowing He shall bring us to a wealthy place of much more than enough. Hallelujah!

David sang praises unto the Lord in the time of trouble. Psalms 27:2-6 says:

When the wicked, even mine enemies
and my foes, came upon me to eat up
my flesh, they stumbled and fell.

Though an host should encamp against me,
my heart shall not fear: though war should
rise against me, in this I will be confident.

One thing have I desired of the LORD,
that will I seek after; that I may dwell
in the house of the LORD all the days of
my life, to behold the beauty of the LORD,
and to enquire in his temple.

For in the time of trouble he shall hide me in
his pavilion: in the secret of his tabernacle shall
he hide me; he shall set me up upon a rock.

And now shall mine head be lifted up above
mine enemies round about me: therefore will
I offer in his tabernacle sacrifices of joy; I will
sing, yea, I will sing praises unto the LORD.

Make up your mind that no matter what comes against you, you'll yet praise the Lord. You may not always be able to praise Him based on what you see. Many times you have to praise Him because of His Word. Your money might be funny. You may be talked about and lied on. You might have some trouble. But continue to praise Him for what His Word says.

SURELY THERE IS AN END

For surely there is an end; and thine
expectation shall not be cut off.
(Prov. 23:18)

The Word of God tells us there is an end to our trials. It doesn't matter what people are going through nor the length of time they've been going through it. It doesn't matter how long people have been in pain, or how long they've been crying because surely there is an end! *And their expectation will not be cut off!* We praise God, not because our trial is over, but because we have an expectation based on the Word of God. We know there's an end to what we're going through. God is bringing us out into a wealthy place (Ps. 66:12).

Sometimes we have to minister to ourselves with the Word of God. We won't get to that "wealthy place" unless we go through. We can make it through when we know there's an end and our expectations will be fulfilled according to the Word of God. We cannot doubt that God will bring us out. We're walking by faith and not by sight (2 Cor. 5:7). We're keeping our expectation because of His Word. Hold fast to your expectation!

NO WEAPON!

No weapon that is formed against thee
shall prosper; and every tongue
that shall rise against thee
in judgment thou shalt condemn.
This is the heritage of the servants
of the LORD, and their righteousness
is of me, saith the LORD.
(Isa. 54:17)

The Word of God tells us that no weapon formed against us shall prosper. The devil may try to destroy us, knock us down, cast us out, crush us, and disturb us. But it won't work! We're going to rise higher than we've ever been.

Whatever the enemy has tried to tear down or destroy, the angels of heaven are empowered to build-up and restore. You must understand your inheritance. The Name of Jesus Christ has *all* power. You may go through a test, but the enemy is a defeated foe. No power of the devil is greater than the power in Jesus Christ's Name (Phil. 2:9–10).

GOD IS ON OUR SIDE

When I was lying sick in my bed, going through one of the toughest times of my life, some angels began to sing a song in my ears. I got up and wrote it down.

If God be for me, who can be against me?
If God is on my side, I cannot be denied
In all these things, we are more than
conquerors, Through Jesus Christ our Lord
And there is nothing that can separate us
From the Love of God

We need to declare to the enemy that we know God is still God and that He is still good. He's blessing us right now! Many years ago there was a song called *Hallelujah Anyhow*. Our problems should never stop us from praising the Lord. When trouble comes our way, we should lift our hands up high and say, "Hallelujah Anyhow!" We are *determined to praise.*

SIX

GET IN POSITION

Before we go further, I want to review the foundational Scriptures for *the blessing of commitment: releasing wealth and riches into your life*. Many times people rush out and try to do something for the Lord without a foundation. But if we don't have a foundation, we cannot stand. We must have the proper foundation to *get in position* and receive God's blessings.

HOLINESS IS A WAY OF LIFE

The first foundational Scripture we studied was Romans 12:1 which reads:

I BESEECH you therefore, brethren,
by the mercies of God, that ye present
your bodies a living sacrifice,
holy, acceptable unto God,
which is your reasonable service.

The Word of God says we must be holy. This Scripture is not referring to a denomination. Holiness is a way of life. Holiness is about us being like God. God is not interested in our fancy clothes or elaborate programs; He's interested in our lifestyle.

We all know plenty of "Sunday Christians." Sunday Christians live one way on Sunday, but Monday through Saturday they lead a different lifestyle. This is not what God is calling for. He's looking for individuals who live holy and glorify Him every day.

Many people believe a lifestyle of holiness is difficult, but the Bible tells us it is the way of transgressors that is difficult (Prov. 13:15). Living holy is not hard once you make up your mind to do so. You *can* live holy if you want to!

Our second foundational Scripture, Romans 12:2 reads:

> *And be not conformed to this world: but be ye transformed by the renewing of your mind, that ye may prove what is that good, and acceptable, and perfect, will of God.*

Commitment to God changes us on the inside. We are transformed and become what God has called us to be. When the world can see Jesus through our lives we can expect blessings to come. We have positioned ourselves to be blessed.

GOD COMMANDS THE BLESSING

When we commit to God, He commands the blessing. We learned about the blessings God has for us in Deuteronomy

28:1–13. God is saying that all we need to do is position ourselves to receive them.

The body of Christ should not be ashamed of being blessed. We should let the world know that we are blessed. There was a time when people would not drive a new car to church because they were afraid the members would criticize them. Many wouldn't tell anyone when they bought a new house, and some were even afraid to wear new clothes. But when we study the Word of God, we understand that we are supposed to have nice things. As long as we're taking care of God's business, He'll take care of ours.

A segment of the church continues to believe they shouldn't be wealthy. I still hear many people in church say, "I don't want it. Just give me a cabin up on a hill. God wants me to be humble."

Well, if you have to live in a cabin on a hill to remain humble that's your problem. But I let God know that whatever He gives me, I'll give Him the glory. I won't get a "big head" because I'm blessed with material things. Whatever I drive, I'll drive in Jesus' Name. Wherever I live, I'll live there in Jesus' Name. Whatever I wear will be worn in Jesus' Name. It's all for His purpose and His Kingdom.

When we see God blessing someone, we shouldn't worry about whether we'll be blessed too. God is searching for people He can use as instruments. When God finds people He can trust to do His work, He'll bless them even more. God wants to hear us say, "Lord we thank you. We're ready to do the work of the Kingdom. We're ready to promote the Gospel of Jesus Christ." We should let God know He can count on us.

GOD GIVES US POWER TO GET WEALTH

Deuteronomy 8:18 taught us:

> *But thou shalt remember the LORD thy God:*
> *for it is he that giveth thee* ***power to get wealth,***
> *that he may establish his covenant which he*
> *sware unto thy fathers, as it is this day.*

We also learned that the blessing of the Lord makes us rich and He adds no sorrow with it (Prov. 10:22). *Wealth and riches* are part of the salvation package. When we give our lives to Christ and receive the baptism of the Holy Ghost, we have positioned ourselves to receive from the Spirit of God. When we get God we get all that He is and everything He stands for.

THE ANOINTING DESTROYS THE YOKE

Next, we went to Isaiah 10:27 which says:

> *And it shall come to pass in that day,*
> *that his burden shall be taken away*
> *from off thy shoulder, and his yoke*
> *from off thy neck, and the yoke shall be*
> *destroyed because of the anointing.*

We saw in this foundational Scripture that the yoke is destroyed because of the anointing. The wonderful thing about the anointing is that it's the same in America, Africa,

Europe, and the rest of the world. Wherever we go, we can stir up the anointing.

Too many Christians, not realizing that they do not have to accept any of the devil's yokes, remain in bondage. Whether it's a yoke of the past, a yoke of guilt, a yoke of addiction or a yoke of debt—the anointing destroys them all.

God doesn't want us to be yoked with anything that prohibits us from going forth and doing His will. We cannot let anything hold us back from doing the work of God. The devil will tell you lies saying, "You can't go anywhere. You can't do anything because of your past." You can tell the devil he's a liar! Your past is under the blood and the blood of Jesus has made you free!

WE MUST BE FAITHFUL

We also studied Hosea 4:6–7 which says:

My people are destroyed for lack
of knowledge: because thou
hast rejected knowledge,
I will also reject thee,
that thou shalt be no priest to me:
seeing thou has forgotten the
law of thy God, I will also
forget thy children.

As they were increased, so they sinned
against me: therefore will I change
their glory into shame.

Here we learned that God's people are destroyed because of the lack of knowledge. The children of Israel rejected knowledge of the Word of God and were not committed to the law of God. The more God blessed them, the more they sinned against Him.

God wants to prosper us, but we must know how to handle prosperity. We must be faithful in giving our tithes and offerings, understanding that everything we have comes from God. When we are faithful with what He has given us, He'll bless us with more.

BLESSED WITH ABRAHAM

We then looked at Genesis 12:2 which reads:

And I will make thee a great nation, and
I will bless thee, and make thy name great;
and thou shalt be a blessing.

Here God commanded blessings upon Abraham. Abraham was blessed not just for his own benefit; he was blessed to be a blessing. To get a better understanding of how the blessings God spoke to Abraham apply to us, we looked at several verses in Galatians 3:7–9, 13–14, 26; and 4:28:

Know ye therefore that they which are of
faith, the same are the children of Abraham.

And the scripture, foreseeing that God
would justify the heathen through faith,
preached before the gospel unto Abraham,
saying, In thee shall all nations be blessed.

So then they which be of faith
are blessed with faithful Abraham.

Christ hath redeemed us from the curse
of the law, being made a curse for us:
for it is written, Cursed is every one
that hangeth on a tree:

That the blessing of Abraham might come on
the Gentiles through Jesus Christ;
that we might receive the promise
of the Spirit through faith.

For ye are all the children of God
by faith in Christ Jesus.

Now we, brethen, as Isaac was,
are the children of promise.

When Jesus endured the cross part of the outcome was that we would receive the blessings God promised to Abraham. Because of Jesus, we are Abraham's seed and heirs according to the promise.

GOD'S DEBT-FREE PLAN

Next, we went to the book of Exodus (see chapters 1–2). The children of Israel had taskmasters who told them when to stand and when to sit. But God brought them out with wealth in their hands. The reason the Egyptians had wealth was for the children of Israel. God gave them a plan to get the silver, gold, and raiment from the Egyptians. When He told the children of Israel to *borrow* these things, the wealth transferred to His people (Ex. 3:20–22).

Realizing they had given away all their wealth and released their laborers, the Egyptians began chasing the children of Israel to bring them back. However, they never caught up with the children of Israel and ended up drowning in the Red Sea. Because there was no one left to pay back, God's people were immediately out of debt. God is ready to *release wealth and riches* to us. While we're praising and glorifying Him, He'll bless us with more than we ever imagined.

The birth of our television ministry at Word of Deliverance is a testimony of God releasing wealth to His people. The initial television equipment we needed cost over $150,000. We planned to make a down payment on the equipment and then secure a loan for the remaining balance.

My wife and I were out of town when God spoke to me and said, "Do not go into debt for that equipment. I'm going to show Myself to the congregation and you are going to pay cash for that equipment." He also said, "Go back and teach this word. I'm going to start releasing money to the people and they are going to bring it for an offering. I will bless them and they shall never be the same."

The members of Word of Deliverance started bringing their offerings for the television equipment. The people brought the money needed to pay for that equipment in cash and we did not go into debt! Initially, our television broadcast, *Taking The Word To The World*, aired on the local community cable network. Today it's televised worldwide. To God be the glory! We're reaching the masses with the gospel of Jesus Christ.

GOD'S PURPOSE

It is important to reiterate that God blesses us so we can support His Kingdom. God reigns and rules over this earth. He promotes His eternal plan. God put money in the children of Israel's hands. He couldn't ask them for an offering unless He provided something for them to give. It's the same today. He puts money in our hands then asks us for not only our tithes, but for an offering as well. Our tithes and offerings bless His work. When we bless His work, we can't help but be blessed.

PRAISE GOD NOW!

We also discussed how the enemy places obstacles in our paths. Some of us may be facing a tragic situation. Tests and trials will come our way, but we must be determined not to let anything stop us from praising God. We were created to worship Him. Our confidence is in who God is, what He said, and what He has promised. We are committed to following His instructions and obeying His commandments. We praise God for what His Word says.

During the time when I first received this word from God on *the blessing of commitment*, a song titled *What God has for Me, It is for Me* was very popular. A member of my congregation who has a program on a local radio station told me, "That song goes with your message." Shortly after that while I was ministering at another church, the bishop there said in his remarks, "What God has for me, it is for me!" I know this was a message from God to me.

What God has for us, it is for us! No one can take it away. The devil can't steal it. This is why we must praise God in the "now time." Praising Him in the now time means regardless of what is happening, how dark things may appear, or how we feel—we must praise Him right now!

We praise God because we know what His Word has declared for us. When the enemy sees us determined to praise God in the now time, he gets confused. He doesn't know what to do with us. He knows it is just a matter of time before he goes down in defeat.

KNOW THE WORD OF GOD

The importance of knowing the Word of God can be seen throughout this teaching. You cannot know God until you know His Word. And when you know the Word of God, you know who you are in Christ. John 6:63 says:

It is the spirit that quickeneth;
the flesh profiteth nothing:
the words that I speak
unto you, they are spirit,
and they are life.

The Word of God is life. The enemy cannot deceive nor destroy you when you know the Word and commit yourself to it. John 8:32 says:

And ye shall know the truth,
and the truth shall make you free.

Knowing the Word of God makes us free! Freedom in God does not come to those who do not seek to know His Word. Making a commitment to God is impossible without making a commitment to knowing His Word.

ARE YOU IN POSITION?

How should we seek God so that we receive all the blessings He has promised us? We should not come to the altar just because the Word of God says He gives us power to get wealth. We should not get on our knees just because we want the Lord to bless us with more money. We already know the Word of God says that the blessing of the Lord makes us rich. It's going to happen because we are positioning ourselves.

People who are in position understand that holiness is a way of life. They faithfully give their tithes and offerings, knowing it all comes from God. Despite life's struggles, they are determined not to let anything or anyone stop their praise. They are committed to studying the Word of God and knowing His will, purpose, and plan for their lives.

Are you in position to receive from the Lord? Ask yourself these questions:

- Am I living holy?
- Do I faithfully give my tithes and offerings?
- Am I determined to praise Him regardless of the circumstances?
- Have I made a commitment to studying and knowing the Word of God?

Honestly reflecting on the above questions can help you pinpoint the areas you need to work on to *get in position.* God will bless you for your commitment. Let's get ready to go deeper into this teaching and learn more about obtaining *the blessing of commitment.*

SEVEN

THE WORD IN US

Thy word have I hid in mine heart,
that I might not sin against thee.
(Ps. 119:11)

The Word was such an important part of David's commitment to God that he laid it in a place where it would always be with him; in his heart. Seeking to have *the Word in us* is not about pleasing people and becoming who they think we should be. This is about pleasing God and becoming who He declares us to be.

Too many Christians grab hold of the Word of God for one minute and let it go the next. One day they're excited, the next day they're apathetic. The only time some Christians pick up a Bible is when they go to church.

The enemy wants us to keep our Bibles closed during service, or even better, leave them at home. He will do anything to try and stop us from getting the Word of God in our hearts. He knows that when we have the Word, there is absolutely no time in our lives when he can have an advantage over us. He tells us, "Don't open your Bible, just sit and listen." But while a student in school, I realized that no matter how smart I was in a particular subject, I could not learn all I needed without my books. Just sitting and listening does not work.

We must be consistent in studying the Word of God *for the blessing of commitment* to flow in our lives. We need His Word in us to fully commit to Him. Let's turn to Joshua, chapter 1, to continue our study. Here the Lord tells Joshua that the children of Israel must obey His commandments and hold onto His Word to have prosperity and success. It reads:

> *Only be thou strong and very courageous,*
> *that thou mayest observe to do according*
> *to all the law, which Moses my servant*
> *commanded thee: turn not from it*
> *to the right hand or to the left,*
> *that thou mayest prosper*
> *whithersoever thou goest.*
>
> *This book of the law shall not depart out of*
> *thy mouth; but thou shalt meditate therein*
> *day and night, that thou mayest observe*
> *to do according to all that is written therein:*
> *for then thou shalt make thy way prosperous,*
> *and then thou shalt have good success.*
> *(Josh. 1:7–8)*

Some people are more familiar with daytime soap operas than the Word of God, but the Bible says we must saturate ourselves with the Word and have it hidden in our hearts. It tells us to meditate on God's Word day and night until it flows out of our mouths. Then, when difficulties arise, we'll have a Word inside reminding us that we don't have to receive the disappointments. We know what the Word of God has promised and remain committed under any circumstance. When the enemy comes, the Word stands against him. The Word in us protects our deliverance.

BECOME A DISCIPLE

Then said Jesus to those Jews which believed
on him, If ye ***continue in my word,***
then are ye my disciples indeed.
(John 8:31)

All over the world churches are filled with people who lack discipline. These individuals are not compelled to study or meditate on the Word of God consistently. When you *continue* in the Word of God, you become a disciple. Disciples are diligent, steadfast, disciplined followers of Christ. As a disciple, you must recognize that the most important thing in your life is following the ways and instructions of God. The only means by which this can be accomplished is to continue in His Word.

Paul followed Jesus' example as he prepared Timothy, his son in the faith, for the ministry. 1 Timothy 4:15–16 says:

Meditate upon these things;
give thyself wholly to them;
that thy profiting may appear to all.

Take heed unto thyself, and unto the doctrine;
continue in them: for in doing this
thou shalt both save thyself,
and them that hear thee.

The promises of God cannot be manifested when we do not continue in the teachings and instructions given to us in the Word. Paul encourages Timothy to continue in the Word of God and lets him know that the blessings he receives for his obedience will be apparent to everyone. He assures Timothy that God's Word will uphold him and equip him to minister to others.

FAIR WEATHER SAINTS

Unfortunately, many Christians are "fair weather saints." Fair weather saints believe God's Word as long as situations in their lives are going well. Mature saints understand that the Word of God helps us in good times and in bad. The Word of God causes us to be planted like a tree by the rivers of water (Ps. 1:3) and we won't be moved no matter what is going on in our lives.

As a pastor, I've learned that observing people's actions is a far better indicator of their commitment than listening to what they say. Many people come to me with a pretty story. They tell me, "I love the Lord and I'm determined to serve Him. If you need me Pastor, just call. I'll do whatever you want. I'll sweep the floor if I have to." Later, when I look for them, I can't find them with a flashlight. Where are they? These individuals always have an excuse: "Bird got out of the cage—I can't go to church!" Fair weather saints are inconsistent because the Word of God is not firmly planted in them.

Internalizing the Word of God is a personal experience. There are times when I want to talk about *Shadrach*, *Meshach* and *Abednego*, but I discovered it's better for me to talk about *your shack!* We need the Word of God in our lives so that our homes will be blessed. Blessings manifest wherever His Word abides.

People have learned how to "have church." We know when to tap our feet, wave our hands, kneel, and stand. We know how to act like we're saved. But if we don't have the Word of God on the inside to keep us, we'll be in trouble by the time we walk outside the church doors.

There has to be something that stays with us when the benediction has been said. His Word does not conclude when church service ends. It keeps on going. It keeps on speaking and standing. It keeps on manifesting because it is His Word.

COUNT IT ALL JOY

My brethren, count it all joy when ye
fall into divers temptations.
(James 1:2)

The Word tells us that no matter what is going on in our lives, we should count it all joy! The only way we can count it all joy is by having the Word of God in our hearts. It is impossible to have joy and praise God in difficult times without knowing what His Word declares. When we know the Word we can sing the song *I've Got A Feeling Everything Is Going To Be All Right*, even when it's raining hell all around us.

Joy is obtained through our spirit, whereas happiness is obtained through our flesh. There's nothing wrong with any of us being happy. However, we must understand the difference between joy and happiness.

Happiness comes from external circumstances or situations. We are happy based on what we receive into our five senses. For example, if someone gives us $50, we're happy. We receive a promotion, we're happy. As long as our bodies feel well, we are happy. But, if no one gives us any money, we are unhappy. When we don't get the promotion and lose the job, we are unhappy. We didn't get the new house, we don't even have a house—we're unhappy! In all of these examples, feeling happy or unhappy depends on external stimuli.

Now let's discuss joy. Joy means *regardless of what we see, feel, hear, taste, or smell, there is a Word of God inside that enables us to give God praise at all times.* Our strength does not come from happiness—the joy of the Lord is our strength!

There have been times in my life when I wanted to give up, but the joy of the Lord bubbling within prompted me to go on. I continued giving God praise. I kept on clapping my hands and standing on the Word of God. Joy brought me where I am today.

AFTER ALL I'VE BEEN THROUGH... I STILL HAVE JOY!

I know how it feels to be sick lying in a hospital bed. I know how it feels to receive a foreclosure notice. I also know how it feels to see my car on a "pick-em-up hook-em-up" tow truck and I didn't call for it. I know what it is like not to have money. There was a time when my marriage was headed for divorce court. But after all I've been through, I still have joy!

The Word of God says, "When the wicked, even mine enemies, and my foes, came upon me to eat my flesh, they stumbled and fell" (Ps. 27:2). We know the enemy wants to destroy us, but a joyful Word from within lets us know that Satan will not win. He has stumbled and fallen.

When people come to me for counseling, I tell them to remember that God is still God. We may not be able to fix every problem or situation but God is still God. As long as we continue to recognize God's sovereignty, we can make it. We know that our trials are working for our good and we will have a testimony of how the devil was defeated. James 1:3–4 says:

Knowing this, that the trying of your faith worketh patience.

But let patience have her perfect work, that ye may be perfect and entire, wanting nothing.

When we have confidence in God's Word, all our needs are met. Why are we whole, lacking nothing? How can we say that after all I've been through, I still have joy? Because the Word is in us and we know God will bless us with everything we need.

GOD CANNOT BLESS A DOUBLE-MINDED PERSON

If any of you lack wisdom, let him ask of
God that giveth to all men liberally,
and unbraideth not; and it shall be given him.

But let him ask in faith, nothing wavering.
For he that wavereth is like a wave of the sea
driven with the wind and tossed.

For let not that man think that he
shall receive any thing of the Lord.

A double minded man is unstable
in all his ways.
(James 1:5–8)

God wants to prosper us, but He cannot bless anyone who is double-minded. Double-minded people are unable to hold firmly onto their belief in the living God. The Word says, "For let not that man think that he shall receive any thing of the Lord" (v. 7). Either we believe in God, or we don't. Either we trust His Word or we don't. A person who waivers back and forth might say, "I sort of believe in God" or "I believe God will do this, but I don't believe God will do that." Double-minded people do not trust God's Word nor understand who He is.

THE WORD IS A CLEANSER

Draw nigh to God, and he will draw nigh to you. Cleanse your hands, ye sinners; and purify your hearts, ye double minded.
(James 4:8)

God's Word must be deep in our hearts, because it is a cleanser. The Word is a purifier. Jesus Himself sanctifies and cleanses us with the washing of water by the Word (Eph. 5:26).

Some Christians are trying to live with an impure heart. Our hearts, minds, ways, and motives must always be pure towards God. Worrying about who likes us is no longer important. It's time to stop trying to win popularity contests. Our focus should be on coming before the Lord with a pure heart.

GET WISDOM

Double-minded people lack wisdom. What is wisdom? It is the proper application or dissemination of knowledge. Proverbs 4:7 tells us:

Wisdom is the principal thing; therefore get wisdom: and with all thy getting get understanding.
(Prov. 4:7)

Many people will say they know something, but have difficulty applying their knowledge. If we have knowledge and don't know how to use it, we won't know how to operate. Once we learn the truth of God's Word, we need wisdom to apply it to our daily lives. Those who do not know how to correctly apply the knowledge of God's Word tend to repeat the same mistakes. For example, if some people were blessed with money today, without wisdom and understanding, many will be broke next week. Let's look again at James 1:8.

If any of you lack wisdom,
let him ask of God, that giveth
to all men liberally, and upbraideth not;
and it shall be given him.

God is generous in giving wisdom to everyone who asks for it. Without wisdom we might end up back in the same pit of debt. We need wisdom to properly handle God's blessing.

Let me give you another example. Some of you will get out of debt. You pay the balance on your bill, but decide to keep the credit card. In August you're shouting, "Glory to God, that bill is paid in full!" In September you're thinking, *Oh, that sure is a nice suit* and charge it. Because you do not have wisdom, by October, you're going to need to be delivered from debt again. You've gone around this mountain long enough—you need wisdom!

Let's turn to 2 Chronicles 1:7 to learn more about wisdom. In this verse God is speaking to someone who would become the wisest man who ever lived. His name was King Solomon.

In that night did God appear
unto Solomon, and said unto him,
Ask what I shall give thee.

Let's imagine God appearing to us in our homes tonight. While we're sitting on our sofas He asks, "What do you want from Me?" God tells us to ask Him for anything we want. What would your answer be? Some might say, "$8,000 or $9,000 would be fine right now." Others might ask for a new house. What should we ask of God?

We must be careful what we ask for because our minds have "little-bitty" ideas. God's thoughts and ways are so much higher than ours. How do we seek God so that every one of His promises will come our way? Let's continue reading.

And Solomon said unto God,
Thou hast showed great mercy unto
David my father, and hast made me
to reign in his stead.

Now, O LORD God, let thy promise unto
David my father be established: for thou
hast made me king over a people
like the dust of the earth in multitude.
(2 Chron. 1:8–9)

King Solomon thought about his spiritual responsibilities. He wanted God to give him the ability to fulfill the purpose He had for his life. Solomon's desire was to be able to carry out the call on his life—a call that was established before the foundation of the earth.

KING SOLOMON ASKS FOR WISDOM

Give me now wisdom and knowledge,
that I may go out and come in before
this people: for who can judge
this thy people, that is so great?
(2 Chron. 1:10)

King Solomon asked God for wisdom and knowledge. In the previous chapter we talked about *getting in position.* King Solomon basically wanted God to put him in the right position and give him the wisdom he needed to deal properly with God's people. He wanted his reign to be pleasing to God. King Solomon understood that God knew more than he did about the task before him.

Like King Solomon, the best thing we can ask of God is for wisdom and knowledge to get in the right position. We need to be in the position where we fulfill God's purpose and will. When we *get in position*, God will bless us beyond our imagination. We'll live in nicer homes than we ever imagined. We'll drive better vehicles and have nicer clothes than we ever dreamed. Therefore, we must be careful not to ask for things that are beneath God's will for us. Anything material we ask God for is really beneath Him; He is so much greater.

We should ask God to put us in the right place so that we can allow His will to come forth and be used in such a time as this. Once we align ourselves with God, the blessing is commanded upon us. 2 Chronicles 1:11–12 says:

And God said to Solomon, Because this was in thine heart, and thou hast not asked riches, wealth, or honour, nor the life of thine enemies, neither yet hast asked long life; but hast asked wisdom and knowledge for thyself, that thou mayest judge my people, over whom I have made thee king:

Wisdom and knowledge is granted unto thee; and I will give thee riches, and wealth, and honour, such as none of the kings have had that have been before thee, neither shall there any after thee have the like.

When we tell God that we want His will to be worked out in our lives, being blessed is our destiny. This includes wealth, riches, health, life and all other blessings that come as a result of our commitment to God.

Many Christians have prayed to God about their finances. When we receive *the blessing of commitment* we are freed from debt. We have money. All of our needs are met. No yoke of the devil is upon us. We're blessed when we come and blessed when we go. All of these blessings are great, but God wants to give us even greater blessings.

Paul wrote in Ephesians 3:20: "Now unto him that is able to do exceeding abundantly above all that we can ask or think." While we're asking God for $1,000, He wants to bless us with $10,000! It's really God's will for these blessings to come to pass, but we must use wisdom with the blessing.

We need wisdom to know how to live a prosperous life acceptable to God. Wisdom teaches us how to act and react in any situation. It enables us to successfully put God's Word to work in our lives. Our financial success has very little to do with our intellectual abilities. We can't do it by ourselves; we must depend on God. By giving us wisdom, He does it for us.

EXPECT TO BE BLESSED

So shall the knowledge of wisdom
be unto thy soul: when thou hast found it,
then there shall be a reward, and thy
expectation shall not be cut off.
(Prov. 24:14)

When we find wisdom, we can expect to be blessed. This Scripture reminds us that *what God has for us, it is for us,* but it takes wisdom to put this statement to work in our lives. When we have wisdom, we know that nothing can stop the blessing.

Wisdom helps us position ourselves to receive from God. When we get wisdom we'll be who God wants us to be, go where He wants us to go, and do what He wants us to do. God's glory will be revealed in our lives.

DON'T MAKE MOSES' MISTAKE

Some people look at their circumstances and get nervous. They look on one side and see a "messed up" situation.

They look over on the other side and see another messed up situation. Leaders look at the people they're trying to minister to and see more mess! But we must be careful not to make the same mistake Moses made. Moses made the mistake of letting the people he was leading get on his nerves. In other words, they made him so angry until he disobeyed God's specific instructions. Anyone who is in a position of leadership has to pray: *God, give me wisdom in dealing with Your people. I want to help Your children, but I need wisdom!*

King Solomon's situation was similar to Moses', but Solomon asked God for wisdom. Because the enemy will bring situations our way that may test our confidence in God, we must continue to ask Him, "Give me wisdom and understanding of how to deal with this situation." When we make this request, God will bless us coming in and going out. Everything our hands touch will be blessed. He'll make us the head and not the tail and place us above and not beneath. He'll cancel our debt. He'll put more money in our hands than we ever had. Wisdom is the principal thing, therefore get wisdom. And with wisdom, get understanding (Prov. 4:7)!

ASK IN FAITH

If any of you lack wisdom,
let him ask of God, that giveth
to all men liberally, and unbraideth not;
and it shall be given him.

*But let him **ask in faith**, nothing wavering.*
For he that wavereth is like a wave of the sea
driven with the wind and tossed.
(James 1:5–6)

It is important that we understand what faith is all about. Without faith, if something happens where it looks like we're going to miss our blessing, we'll start panicking. With faith we can stand calmly because we trust God's Word. Whatever His Word says is true, even if it is beyond our comprehension. That's when we know it's really God—when it's beyond us. Hebrews 11:1 tells us:

NOW *faith is the substance*
of things hoped for, the evidence
of things not seen.

Most people who have attended church have heard about faith, but there are still many people who really don't understand it. Faith keeps us from being double-minded. Faith keeps us standing and believing the Word that we received. Faith is what brings things not seen into the present. "Now faith" is the reason we can praise God right now! We can rejoice because we know, through faith, everything He has promised is coming forth. Every seed we've sown shall bring forth a harvest.

Faith must be at work in us for *the blessing of commitment that releases wealth and riches into our lives* to be manifested. This is not about the world looking at us and seeing how wonderful we are. When the world sees us blessed they're really looking at what God has done.

WHAT WILL BE ALREADY IS

Faith is a spiritual thing. It's faith that lets us call those things that are not in the natural as though they were, because they are in the spiritual. Several years ago I preached a message called *What Will Be Already Is*. Faith lets us know that what will be already is. It may not have manifested in the natural realm, but everything God has promised has already taken place in the spirit realm. When Jesus said, "It is finished," He meant it. That's why I can tell people who are sick that they're already healed. They may ask, "But what if I still have pain in my body?" I tell them, "You're still healed!" A Word was spoken for our healing over 2000 years ago. We need faith to connect what's happening with our bodies with the Word that has already been spoken for us. Then we can experience the manifestation in the natural because in the spirit *it is already so*.

BLOOD-WASHED, BLOOD-BOUGHT, SANCTIFIED, HOLY GHOST-FILLED, CHILD OF THE LIVING GOD!

We must learn to live according to what the Word of God has declared for us. We know what God has spoken by studying His Word. When people see your head held high and a confident look on your face, and they know you don't have any money, they wonder, *Who do you think you are?* You can tell them you're a blood-washed, blood-bought, sanctified, Holy Ghost-filled, child of the living God! We have His Word deep inside us. We know what Deuteronomy, chapter 28, promises to those who are committed to Him. We are who God says we are and we're going where He says we're going.

Start getting excited about God's promises. When your monthly bank statement comes, though it may show a balance of only $20, pick up that statement and shout, "Glory to God. The Holy Ghost is getting ready to add more zeros to my balance!"

DO A FAITH THING!

But without faith it is impossible
to please him: for he that cometh
to God must believe that he is,
and that he is a rewarder
of them that diligently seek him.
(Heb. 11:6)

We sing a song at Word of Deliverance written by my brother, Chris Hilton, titled *Do a Faith Thing!* More people would feel better, look better, and have a better outlook on life if they did a "faith thing."

By faith we stand on the Word of God. By faith we are who God says we are. By faith we are able to do what we do. We are *the called of God*, by faith. We are *the anointed of God*, by faith. By faith we are *the sons of God*; no longer servants, but sons. By faith we inherit every promise of God. By faith His glory is being revealed in our lives. We are feeding faith to this Word on *the blessing of commitment*, because we know the just shall live by faith (Rom. 1:17, Gal. 3:11, Heb. 10:38). Faith cometh by hearing and hearing by the Word of God (Rom. 10:17). *Wealth and riches* shall be in our homes, by faith. All of it happens by faith.

Faith is our spiritual arm, eye, and ear. It's our spiritual taster, smeller, and feeler. And since the world is more spiritual than natural, faith has the upper hand. We can kneel on the altar day and night and pray for faith, but it's not going to come that way. The Word of God feeds our faith. We must study the Word and find out what it says concerning our blessings. The Word says we are wealthy and rich (Ps. 112:3), and healed (Isa. 53:4). It also says we are delivered (Ps. 34:19). The more we meditate on the Word of God, the more our faith increases. *The blessing of commitment*, by faith, is coming forth for the glory of God.

Faith makes us whole and complete. The transforming of our minds we discussed previously can only happen by faith. We literally have to change our ways and attitudes by faith. This allows God to transform us into who He called us to be for His purpose.

The Lord may call you to do a task for His Kingdom that is impossible to accomplish without faith. You want to tell the Lord, "I'm not sure I can do this. Jesus, the idea is wonderful, but do you really want me to do this by faith?" You must get to the point where you tell the Lord, "Yes, I'll go. I believe you have invested and planted in me everything it takes to accomplish what you have called and ordained for me to do."

The Word in Us guides us in fulfilling God's purpose and will for our lives. We need to ask God for direction because we can't direct ourselves. We need to ask Him to order our steps because we can't do it. Like King Solomon, we need to let the Lord know that we realize we're not intelligent enough to do His business.

God wants to do so much for us. He is ready to *release wealth and riches into our lives*. He has already done so many wonderful and marvelous things. Let's *do a faith thing* and humble ourselves before Him. May God grant unto us the wisdom to do His will.

EIGHT

SPIRITUAL COMMITMENT

Thou shalt arise, and have mercy upon Zion:
for the time to favour her,
yea, the set time, is come.
When the LORD shall build up Zion,
he shall appear in his glory.
(Ps. 102:13,16)

Let's make the above Scriptures personal by replacing Zion with your name. If you are male, change her to him. Now when you read these Scriptures you know the Lord is talking about you! He's building you up for His glory. You're under construction. This is the *set time* and it is your time now. Let us bless the name of the Lord.

For most of us, the more we learn about the *blessing of commitment*, the more we want to do what is right concerning the things of God. Some people may be planning to study the Bible more often while others may be concentrating on getting more involved in a particular ministry. We want to "step up" our level of commitment because we understand there is a blessing in being committed.

We promise to go to church not only on Sundays, but also on Wednesday nights for Bible study. We get so excited about the blessings we start "moon walking" during service. Unfortunately, after a week or two, some of us return to our old habits. We're at church, then we're not. We're up and then we're down. We're in and then we're out. What is the problem? It was a *flesh commitment*.

We are composed of spirit, soul, and body. Whatever we do for the Lord must be done from our spirit. When we try to do something for the Lord with our bodies (flesh), we tend to get tired and sit down. But when we make a *spiritual commitment*, we determine to do something out of our passion to please God. We stick with it and our spirit hangs in there because it knows there is a reward for being committed.

SPIRIT VERSUS FLESH

This I say then, Walk in the Spirit,
and ye shall not fulfil the lust of the flesh.
(Gal. 5:16)

It is important that we understand the difference between spirit and flesh. The flesh is not saved; it's the spirit that is Holy Ghost-filled. In this Scripture, we are instructed to *Walk in the Spirit*. To walk in the Spirit literally means to exist, abide, or live according to the Word of God at all times. We must give our spirit priority over our flesh, presenting our bodies as a living sacrifice (Rom. 12:1). Our bodies remain under subjection to the Spirit of God that dwells in us.

> *For they that are after the flesh do mind the things of the flesh; but they that are after the Spirit the things of the Spirit.*
> *(Rom. 8:5)*

We need to be aware of how the flesh operates. The flesh always wants to go after the things that are against the Spirit or contrary to God's Word. It wants us to do the things that please the flesh. But we must be determined to do the things that are profitable to the spirit man.

We don't have to learn how to operate in the flesh—we're born knowing how to do it. The flesh works through our body gates. The eye gate sees a problem and we start worrying. The ear gate hears some bad news and we get discouraged. Because it cannot touch the spiritual, the feel gate has us doubting that our blessings will come to pass. The flesh also operates through the smell gate and the taste gate. Part of walking in the Spirit is learning how to keep the flesh with its body gates under subjection to the Spirit of God. This means we never allow our flesh to do anything outside the boundaries of His Word, no matter what is going on.

It's fairly easy for us to keep our flesh under control when we're around people who are spiritual. The difficulty comes when we have to deal with people who are "in the world." Being saved and born again does not remove us from the problems and troubles that come from living in this world.

But we handle these situations the way the Spirit, not the flesh, would have us handle them. When we were in the world, if someone got under our skin, we had one type of reaction. But now that we're walking in the Spirit we react differently.

The Lord will teach us how to crucify our flesh. Things that bothered me five years ago do not bother me anymore. The Lord allowed the same thing to happen to me repeatedly until I learned how to handle it. The same test will be presented to us again and again until we pass it!

We don't have time to fight over silly stuff. We have to learn to tell ourselves it isn't worth it. It feels so much better praising God. Things turn out better when we put our energy into praising Him. Let's continue reading Romans, chapter 8.

For to be carnally minded is death;
but to be spiritually minded is life and peace.

Because the carnal mind is enmity against
God: for it is not subject to the law of God,
neither indeed can be.

So then they that are in the flesh
cannot please God.
(Rom. 8:6–8)

The mind of the flesh (carnal mind) opposes God and leads to death spiritually, emotionally, physically, and financially. To be spiritually-minded brings life and peace. A carnal-minded person cannot submit to the Word of God. John 6:63 lets us know that God's Word is spirit and life. His

Word transforms us through our spirit. Everything about pleasing God is spiritual, therefore, it is impossible for those who are in the flesh to please Him.

Our spirit and flesh are at war with each other. When we accepted Jesus Christ as our personal Lord and Savior, the devil lost his position. He is no longer in control of our bodies, actions, thoughts, ways, or motives. All that we are belongs to God. The enemy is always around ready and waiting for the opportunity to get his place back in your life. There's always a battle and a struggle. But when you give God's Spirit total rule over your life the devil will always be defeated.

CHRIST DWELLS IN US

But ye are not in the flesh, but in the Spirit,
if so be that the Spirit of God dwell in you.
Now if any man have not
the Spirit of Christ, he is none of his.
(Rom. 8:9)

When we are *in the Spirit*, Christ dwells in us. If the Spirit of God is not alive in us, we don't belong to God. If we don't belong to God we cannot be subject to His Word, neither can we be committed to Him.

And if Christ be in you,
the body is dead because of sin;
but the Spirit is life
because of righteousness.
(Rom. 8:10)

When Christ is in us, the body or flesh is no longer in charge; the Spirit is in charge. The Spirit frees us from the bondage of sin and makes it possible for us to have total deliverance. Unfortunately, many times people fall back into sin because they're trying to maintain their deliverance in the flesh. But our deliverance is kept through the power of the Holy Spirit.

There is never any acceptable reason to sin. Everything we do must give God glory. Trusting God's Word and doing things His way is sometimes a struggle, especially when we don't feel confident about the outcome of a particular situation. But *spiritual commitment* is not about how we feel; it's about having absolute trust in an absolute God. If we operated according to how we felt, we would never be committed.

SONS OF GOD

But if the Spirit of him that raised up Jesus
from the dead dwell in you,
he that raised up Christ from the dead
shall also quicken your mortal bodies
by his Spirit that dwelleth in you.

Therefore, brethren, we are debtors,
not to the flesh, to live after the flesh.

For if ye live after the flesh,
ye shall die: but if ye
through the Spirit do mortify the deeds
of the body, ye shall live.

For as many as are led by the Spirit of God,
they are the sons of God.
(Rom. 8:11–14)

When the Spirit leads us, we are sons of God and His blessings are commanded upon us. Being called a "son" in these Scriptures has nothing to do with a person's gender. This is about our position with God as our Heavenly Father.

For ye have not received the spirit of bondage
again to fear; but ye have received
the Spirit of adoption,
whereby we cry, Abba, Father.
(Rom. 8:15)

God is our Father. When we cry out, "Father, Father," we're getting personal. As long as we try to worship God in the flesh we'll never get to the place of having a personal relationship with Him. "God is Spirit: and they that worship Him must worship Him in spirit and in truth" (John 4:24). Only when we worship Him in spirit and receive His Spirit can we say, "He's my Father."

The Spirit itself beareth witness with our
spirit, that we are the children of God:

And if children, then heirs; heirs of God,
and joint-heirs with Christ;
if so be that we suffer with him,
that we may be also glorified together.
(Rom. 8:16–17)

Being heirs of God means that whatever belongs to Him belongs to us. The inheritance flows down. The promises we've been learning about come forth through the spirit, not the flesh. The flesh will "act up." When it's time to go to church the flesh says, "I'm not going; it's too hot! I'm not going; it's too cold! I'm not going; it's raining too hard! I'm not going; it's too dry!" But our spirit understands that God is still on the throne. Our spirit wants to do whatever it takes to please God, and thereby be His heirs. As heirs, spiritual rain pours down on us and spiritual power is at work inside us.

WAIT ON THE PROMISES OF GOD

For I reckon that the sufferings
of this present time are not worthy
to be compared with the glory
which shall be revealed in us.
(Rom. 8:18)

Many of us have suffered from painful experiences. However, the Word tells us that our suffering cannot be compared with the glory that will be revealed through us to the world. No matter what I may be going through, I've learned to wait on the promises of God. I know God will take me through and He'll bring me out.

There may have been times when you have wondered, like I have, *Lord, why me? I'm trying to do the best I can. I'm trying to live right. I don't bother anyone. I'm trying to walk upright. Why me? I don't go to nightclubs. I don't drink. I don't smoke. Lord, why me?* But the Word tells us if we suffer with Him, we'll reign with Him (2 Tim. 2:12).

The same people who saw us when we were down, will see us rise. That's when His glory will be revealed in us. Weeping may endure for a night (a season), but joy (God's revelation) comes in the morning (Ps. 30:5).

THINK YOURSELF HAPPY

We'll find ourselves much better off when we determine within ourselves that no matter what we must deal with, we are going to dwell in the goodness of God. We need to do as Paul did when he had to defend himself before King Agrippa. Paul was in a difficult situation. The chief priests and their followers were angry with him for preaching the gospel of Jesus Christ. They told all kinds of lies about Paul and had him put in prison. Even though Paul had been found innocent of any wrongdoing, the Jewish leaders still wanted him put to death.

How did Paul respond in a situation where his enemies wanted him dead? He began his testimony to King Agrippa saying, "I think myself happy" (Acts 26:2). In other words, Paul chose to think on God's goodness. He used this difficult situation as an opportunity to share his faith. We must learn how to "think ourselves happy." We can pout if we choose, but I'm a witness it doesn't do any good. It's better to lift up our heads, hearts, and spirits to praise God again because this stirs up the spirit man.

Paul gives similar advice to the believers at Philippi as he encourages them to be steadfast and of the same mind in the Lord. Philippians 4:8 says:

Finally, brethren, whatsoever things are true, whatsoever things are honest, whatsoever things are just, whatsoever things are pure, whatsoever things are lovely, whatsoever things are of good report; if there be any virtue, and if there be any praise, think on these things.

When our spirits have this attitude and mind-set, the flesh can't handle it. Our troubles may weigh heavily on us, but the Word says:

For our light affliction, which is but for a moment, worketh for us a far more exceeding and eternal weight of glory;
(2 Cor. 4:17)

It's just a light affliction and only for a moment. Soon, God will deliver us!

CREATION IS WAITING ON US

For the earnest expectation of the creature waiteth for the manifestation of the sons of God.
(Rom. 8:19)

Creation is waiting on us to return to our spiritual position as sons of God. When man sinned, the earth and all creation was cursed. The flowers and grass in our yards and the trees by our windows are waiting for us to take our position as sons. All creation knows who God is; and the Word of God says that if we don't praise Him, the rocks will (Luke 19:40).

For we know that the whole creation
groaneth and travaileth in pain
together until now.
(Rom. 8:22)

Because creation was cursed, there is a travailing and groaning in the earth. When man sinned, all creation lost its place spiritually. But as man moves back to his place with God, the spiritual effect flows throughout the earth.

Before we cleared the land to build Word of Deliverance church, I frequently would drive by the property at night. At that time there were many trees and bushes on the property. Often I would drive down Southland Road and hear the praises of God surrounding this land. On one occasion I had to go around the block and turn around. I thought I heard the bushes say, "Hallelujah!"

When you are going through a test, try looking out your window. You'll see creation waving its hands. You'll hear trees saying, "Glory to the Most High God!" Even creation knows how to come forth with praise.

MOVE IN THE SPIRIT

Because we know what has already been spoken in the spirit shall be manifested, we're optimistic about our future. Someone's marriage may be in trouble. Parents may not know where their child is. But Romans 4:17 tells us "Even God, ...calleth those things which be not as though they were."

It takes *moving in the spirit* to believe in something that has not yet manifested in the natural. The flesh cannot do it. In the flesh it is impossible for a wife to look at her husband, who at one time treated her badly; and tell him he's wonderful and that she is glad to have him in her life. In the flesh a husband cannot look at his wife, who previously caused him pain and tell her that she's beautiful and the best thing that ever happened to him. But when we move in the spirit we can look at our spouse and say, "Baby! Baby! Baby! I feel something for you like I never felt before." It's a spiritual thing.

Moving in the spirit allows us to look at a zero bank account balance and speak to it according to the Word of God that says wealth and riches shall be in our house. We no longer worry or fret about our children because moving in the spirit allows us to abide in God's peace. When we feel like we are fainting and everything in the natural indicates a situation is hopeless; a Word will come out of our spirit telling us that after we have done all we can, just stand (Eph. 6:13).

WHOSE REPORT WILL YOU BELIEVE?

Either we believe the report of the Lord or we believe the report of the flesh. The natural side says give up. The natural side says we should quit. The natural side says it's over. The problem that entered through the body gates tells us that moving in the spirit wouldn't work. But the Holy Ghost says it's not over until God says its over!

If you are having difficulty declaring and holding on to the promise of God's Word, read and confess Scripture until it strengthens your spirit. Remember, faith increases by hearing the Word of God (Rom. 10:17).

Some people attend church and pretend to have it all together. We don't have to pretend. If the Lord had not been on our side, I don't know where any of us would be. We're never too sanctified and holy to get on the altar and ask the Lord for help. Jesus will help us. He'll push and lift us when we come and empty out ourselves before Him. He doesn't care about our diplomas or degrees. All we have to do is ask Him for what we need. I John 5:14–15 says:

And this is the confidence that we have
in him, that, if we ask any thing
according to his will, he heareth us:

And if we know that he hear us,
whatsoever we ask, we know that we have
the petitions that we desired of him.

We are sons of God. We've made a *spiritual commitment.* We refuse to allow the things that come through our body gates to control our lives. The enemy may try to talk to our minds, but we talk back to him using the Word of God, letting him know we're not worried. We must stand on God's Word and believe His report. We're still under construction and when God is through with us, we shall come forth as pure gold (Job 23:10).

NINE

SPIRITUAL ADULTERY

Many Christians are spiritual adulterers. When people hear the word *adultery*, they most often think about sexual things. Of course, those who are involved in any type of sexual relationship outside their marriage and violate the Word of God are committing a type of spiritual adultery. But *spiritual adultery* in our relationship with God goes beyond sexual improprieties. Christians commit spiritual adultery when they say they're part of the body of Christ, yet do things that are contrary to Him and His instructions.

It doesn't take a long analytical process to determine if the things we are doing are pleasing to God. Sometimes we try to make God more complicated than He is. We know if we're not walking or talking right. For example, if a believer mistreats his neighbor, then goes to church waving his hands and shouting Hallelujah—that's spiritual adultery. A coworker pretends everything is fine and wonderful and says she loves the Lord, yet she knows she is causing all kinds of problems in her workplace. That woman is committing spiritual adultery.

At first when believers begin to go astray, there is a check or nudge in their spirit because the Holy Ghost reveals all truth (see John 14:26). Unfortunately, after awhile, some get comfortable with committing spiritual adultery. They think they are getting away with what they're doing and that it's all right. But the Bible says we will know them by their fruits (Matt. 7:20). People bring forth the "fruit" of the spirit they have been intimate with. When people are intimate with a spirit other than the Lord's, their fruit will not be of Him.

Surprisingly, many spiritual adulterers think they are going to heaven. I must tell people the truth. When death comes, if you don't live right, you'll see a flash of light. But it will not be a light from heaven; it will be the fire of hell! God is calling for people who will do more than just "talk the talk." We must "walk the walk" and be an example of who God is. To receive *the blessing of commitment,* we must obey His commandments and allow His Word to flourish in our lives.

If the church is not careful the enemy will set up camp right in our midst. This happened to the children of Israel during the time when Joshua was their leader. God had given the children of Israel instructions on what not to touch, take or do in the land He had promised them. God was with them and He gave Joshua and the children of Israel mighty victories over their enemies. But then one of the Israelites named Achan disobeyed God's instructions and took things from the spoils forbidden by Him. The Lord became angry with the children of Israel, and consequently when they went to battle against the men of Ai, they were defeated. Joshua and all Israel stoned Achan and his family to death. They set them on fire and burned up everything the man owned (see Joshua, chapter 7).

1-900-KNEE

Touching that which is forbidden usually happens gradually. People will pick up a little here and there, and dabble in this and that. Today's psychic hotlines are a good example. People think it's okay to call "900" telephone numbers to talk with psychics, but when Christians need a "word" we better get on our "1-900-KNEE!"

It is a dangerous situation when people think they can be in the body of Christ while committing spiritual adultery. God is not going to allow anyone to continue to violate Him because His will and purpose cannot come forth through an adulterous person. The Lord wants to deliver us so that His glory is revealed in our lives.

This does not mean someone who has committed spiritual adultery should stop going to church. Everyone is welcome in the house of God, and that includes people with nontraditional lifestyles or those who may be suffering from different types of addictions or abnormal behaviors. Many people come into the house of God in a manner not pleasing to Him. However, He does not intend for us to continue that way. Unfortunately, many who have not yet come into the "newness of life" are in church serving as ushers, choir members, or even as ministerial staff members. This is not the time to be serving, but rather the time to be on the altar praying on our "1-900-KNEE."

DEPARTING FROM THE LORD

The beginning of the word of the LORD
by Hosea. And the LORD said to Hosea,
Go, take unto thee a wife of
whoredoms and children of whoredoms:
for the land hath committed great whoredom,
departing from the LORD.
(Hos. 1:2)

In this Scripture the Lord tells the prophet Hosea that the people are committing whoredom. In other words, the people were departing from the Lord. When people depart from God, most times they do not run away from Him. Instead, it is done gradually. Little by little losing their spiritual commitment and bringing forth a spirit that is not of God.

BACKSLIDERS

When the Lord spoke to Hosea about people of whoredoms, He wasn't talking about people "in the world." He was talking about His people committing whoredom. The people were retreating from the principles, ways, and instructions of the Lord. They were "backsliding." Backsliders are spiritual adulterers.

Backsliding doesn't start when someone decides they will no longer attend church. From my pastoral experience, most backsliders I have known stay in the church for approximately three to six months before they stop attending completely. Backsliding starts in the mind and people keep entertaining these thoughts while gradually getting further away from God. After awhile, nothing about the church sounds, looks, or feels good to them. They forget that God is still God. They have departed from the instructions and ways of the Lord.

GOD EXTENDS MERCY TO PRAISERS

But I will have mercy upon the house of Judah, and will save them by the LORD their God, and will not save them by bow, nor by sword, nor by battle, by horses, nor by horsemen.
(Hos. 1:7)

Thank God for His mercy. God tells Hosea that He will have mercy upon the house of Judah. In Scripture the house of Judah refers to a house of praise. In other words, His mercy is upon those who will give Him praise.

The Lord will not accept just any kind of praise. We must come before Him in the right spirit, then we can offer up "real praise." It takes a *right spirit* to have real praise. Real praise has power. When we have real praise and keep on praising Him, something marvelous is going to happen. Praise stirs up the anointing and the anointing destroys yokes. When the *wrong spirit* is in the house of God, instead of the praise going higher, that spirit hinders our praise.

The enemy's goal is to keep us from praising and worshipping God with the right spirit. He doesn't care if thousands of people call themselves Christians as long as their spirit is not right. It doesn't matter to him whether or not we go to church, as long as our spirit is not right. He knows that when our spirit isn't right, we won't treat each other as we should and we won't love one another.

SEARCH ME LORD

It is very important for all of us to take a personal inventory. We're in a dangerous mind-set when we cannot examine ourselves and ask God to search us. Sometimes we're so busy knowing what's wrong with someone else, we forget about "checking" ourselves.

I've had many people tell me over the years that they want to be sure they are in the right place with God. The Bible contains many prayers, but there are two that I refer to when this issue comes up. The first one, from Psalm 139, is a prayer of humility:

Search me, O God,
and know my heart:
try me, and know my thoughts:

And see if there be any wicked way in me,
and lead me in the way of everlasting.
(Ps. 139:23–24)

This is an effective prayer for times when we want to say, "God, I want to be right and I want to be whole. Search me Lord." We must be sincere when we ask the Lord to search us because He may show us some things about ourselves we don't like. When the Lord shows some of us our ways, and it's a terrible picture, we're tempted to say, "That's not me!" However, when we ask God to search us, we must accept what He shows.

BE SURE YOUR SIN WILL FIND YOU OUT!

The second prayer I refer to is a very popular prayer of repentance. This prayer is found in Psalm 51. The enemy wants us to get comfortable in our wrongdoing. He leads people to believe that no one will ever know about it. He wants us to forget that the Word of God says, "...and be sure your sin will find you out" (Num. 32:23b).

David wrote Psalm 51 because he got caught. Most Christians are familiar with the story of David and Bath-sheba (see 2 Samuel, chapters 11–12). It all started when David, while relaxing on the roof of his palace, looked down and saw a beautiful woman bathing. David thought, *M'm! M'm! M'm! Good!* He said, "I want to know her name" and sent his people to find out about this woman. David's people told him the woman's name was Bath-sheba and that she was married to Uriah, a soldier in the king's army. They told him that Uriah was away fighting in the war. David sent for Bath-sheba and he lay with her.

David thought everything was fine even though he had committed adultery. Then he found out Bath-sheba was pregnant! Now David had to come up with a scheme to hide the fact that he was the father. To cover up his sin he decided to send for Uriah from the war so that Uriah would lay with Bath-sheba.

David had Uriah brought to his palace. He questioned Uriah on how the war was going and encouraged him to go home and "be" with his wife, but Uriah would not go. He pretty much said, "Not tonight, I don't feel like it. I can't do this while my friends are still on the battlefield."

David had to come up with another plan. He had Uriah put on the front line of the worst battle so that Uriah would be killed. David thought his problems were over. He continued on his happy-go-lucky way! He was still carrying out his duties. He was still "churchin." Still singing and praising the Lord. He thought, *I got away with that one!*

The Lord sent the prophet Nathan to confront David about his sin. Nathan told David a story about a rich man who had many flocks and herds. This rich man took the one lamb that belonged to a poor man. When Nathan finished the story, David said that whoever would do something like that should surely die. Nathan the prophet told David, "Thou art the man" (2 Sam.12:7). I believe David probably fell to his knees and said, "Ahh...."

This is when David wrote Psalm 51 which begins with David crying out, "Have mercy upon me, O God" (Ps. 51:1). David acknowledged his sin and repented.

DON'T DO IT!

The moral failures that have exploded throughout the church community must be checked. Week after week we hear of leaders who have become entrapped in adulterous affairs, many leading to divorce. The devil has used man's weakness for women since the beginning of time to take men out of position. We must recognize this and be determined not to allow our marriages or ministries to become another scandal and embarrassment to the body of Christ!

It's time to make up your mind to live right, because if you don't, you're going to get busted! There's no need for people to have their mouths wide open, looking surprised and dumbfounded when they get caught. The best thing is: *don't do it!*

CREATE IN ME A CLEAN HEART, RENEW A RIGHT SPIRIT WITHIN ME

I encourage people to get their lives right before they have to write a Psalm like Psalm 51. I prayed Psalm 51 before I started in the ministry. If we find ourselves out of place with God, we need to learn how to quickly get back in place. David cried out to God and asked Him to create a clean heart and renew a right spirit within him (v.10).

We cannot continue being intimate with the wrong spirit. We cannot allow that spirit to keep manifesting and take us away from the ways of God. We must consistently make sure our spirits are clean and purged before the Lord.

THE DEVIL GOES TO CHURCH TOO!

And no marvel; for Satan himself
is transformed into an angel of light.
(2 Cor. 11:14)

Many people don't realize that the devil gets up on Sunday morning; puts on a suit, shirt, and tie, carries a Bible and a briefcase, and goes to church. Sometimes he has on a robe or a dress and he wears fine shoes. The enemy comes to church so often, he even knows the Word of God! He loves church. Satan loves to sing, play musical instruments, and usher. One pastor told me that sometimes the devil even transforms himself into a holiness preacher!

The adversary can do everything believers can except live right. This is why God is not impressed with people just because they go to church. Many people go to church with the wrong spirit. We must ask ourselves if our spirit is right before God, and if He is getting glory out of every area and situation in our lives.

TRY THE SPIRITS

BELOVED, believe not every spirit,
but try the spirits whether they are of God:
because many false prophets
are gone out into the world.
(1 John 4:1)

In this Scripture the apostle John admonishes the church to "try" the spirits. *Try* here means to test how true something is based on the Word of God. We might ask, "What is the real motive behind what is happening? Who is positioned to receive glory from this situation?"

The church exists to do the work of the Lord. God is not going to allow any work that He purposed to be done be hindered by those whose spirits are not right. We must try the spirits because many false prophets, preachers, and teachers have gone out into the world. We must be sure the spirits at work are of God, realizing the devil goes to church too.

WHAT IS YOUR MOTIVE?

THOUGH I speak with the tongues
of men and of angels,
and have not charity,
I am become as sounding brass,
or a tinkling cymbal.
(1 Cor. 13:1)

Charity in the above Scripture means love. Love should always be the motive in serving the Lord. It's all to His glory. There are Christians all over the world distraught because they did something in the wrong spirit and with the wrong motive. Instead of wanting the glory directed towards God, they want it directed towards them.

These people get upset when the pastor doesn't mention their name. If they're on a committee, they want everyone to be aware of their contribution. If they're in the choir, they resent someone else being chosen to sing a solo and will not clap for them. They won't attend an event when their names aren't on the program. They become frustrated and join with others like themselves, refusing to talk to anyone in the church who is not a part of their group!

If left unchecked, wrong spirits will stir up division in the church. Committees, sections, and segments start choosing sides and cliques begin to develop. They don't understand that the real question is "Are you on the Lord's side? When we are on the Lord's side, it no longer matters whose group we're in. All that matters is that God is glorified.

When people operate with the wrong spirit, they make themselves susceptible to all kinds of attacks from the enemy. They're open to constantly feeling insulted and offended. They forget that the important thing is to let God be glorified.

God is not concerned about our *spiritual resumés*. A lot of Christians keep a long list of everything they've ever done for the church. They worked on this committee or sat on this board. They organized a bake sale or sold tickets to a program. They think their spiritual resumé gives them a Holy Ghost connection with God. But if any of these things were done with the wrong spirit, they have not done a thing.

When we do something in the church, it is not important who gets the credit. The important thing is that the will and purpose of God be accomplished. When we operate in this spirit, men and women will see God's glory through our lives. God is calling for those who are committed to staying in the right position and in right standing with Him. As long as our motives are right, He will bless us for our commitment.

OPERATING WITH THE RIGHT SPIRIT

When the church operates with the right spirit, God moves and marvelous things happen. Our level of motivation becomes so high that when the enemy attacks us, we can handle it. Let's go to the book of Acts to see what happens when we operate at this level.

And believers were the more added
to the Lord, multitudes both
of men and women.
(Acts 5:14)

These believers were having some church! The Holy Ghost was moving. An enormous number of men and women were coming to the Lord being saved. They were having a wonderful time.

Insomuch that they brought forth
the sick into the streets, and laid them
on beds and couches, that at the least
the shadow of Peter passing by
might overshadow some of them.

There came also a multitude out of
the cities round about Jerusalem,
bringing sick folks, and them which
were vexed with unclean spirits:
and they were healed every one.
(Acts 5:15–16)

All who came to the church needing healing were healed. Those vexed with unclean spirits were delivered—every single one of them. The church was experiencing a powerful move of God.

THE DEVIL TRIES TO SLIP IN

Then the high priest rose up,
and all they that were with him,
(which is the sect of the Sadducees,)
and were filled with indignation
(Acts 5:17)

The high priest and his followers were upset. They heard about the wonderful things happening in the church, and became angry because they had not been part of it. We must never think, even in an atmosphere where God is moving, that the devil is not going to try and slip in.

I can imagine the high priest saying, "How could they have such a wonderful time when I wasn't preaching?" He became indignant and wanted to put an end to it. Even today, some preachers don't think there can be a wonderful service unless they are preaching. They don't want to hear about people being healed if the people weren't in their prayer line.

Whenever we are involved in work for the Lord, the enemy is going to point weapons straight at us. The Bible does not say that weapons would not be formed against us. It says those weapons would not prosper. We know that God has angels encamped round about His people who fear Him (Ps. 34:7). Therefore, any fiery dart the devil points at us will be quenched (Eph. 6:16).

WHO WERE THE SADDUCEES?

The high priest and his followers were Sadducees. The Sadducees were Jews who did not believe that Jesus Christ was the Messiah. They also did not believe in the resurrection of the dead, angels, or demons (Acts 23:8). The Sadducees didn't want to hear all those testimonies that came along with the preaching of the gospel. Let's look at a few more verses from Acts, chapter 5, to see what the Sadducees planned to do about the apostles.

Verse 18:

And laid their hand on the apostles,
and put them in the common prison.

The high priest had the apostles put in the common prison where the worst criminals were kept. But the apostles didn't get nervous. They knew God was going to show up.

Verse 19:

But the angel of the Lord by
night opened the prison doors,
and brought them forth, and said,

This is an example of what we mean when we sing, "Late in the midnight hour, God's going to turn it around!" That night, the angel of the Lord opened the prison doors. If we keep the praise going, an Angel is going to come and let us out!

Verses 20–23:

Go, stand and speak in
the temple to the people
all the words of this life.

And when they heard that, they entered into the temple early in the morning, and taught. But the high priest came, and they that were with him, and called the council together, and all the senate of the children of Israel, and sent to the prison to have them brought.

But when the officers came, and found them not in the prison, they returned, and told,

Saying, The prison truly found we shut with all safety, and the keepers standing without before the doors: but when we had opened, we found no man within.

When the high priest sent his people to get the apostles, they were already gone. They were in the temple, boldly teaching the people. The enemy's plan was to put the apostles in prison, but God had a different plan.

The devil's tactics have not changed. He's still determined to put all of us in prison spiritually, mentally, and/or physically. He still sends his spirits to tell lies on us and disrupt our finances. He even tries to send sickness our way. He uses these types of things to put us into a little demon's prison. The situations he placed in our homes were sent to imprison us. The problems he put on our jobs are there to imprison us. But when we get in that prison, we can't allow him to hinder our praise. We must keep on praising God.

This is why it's so important to have the right spirit. If we don't have the right spirit, when these things happen we will get mad at God. Some will say, "I can't believe God allowed this to happen to me! Hard as I work in the ministry, how could He let this thing stir up?" But when the enemy comes to entangle us, what we should be saying is "Hallelujah anyhow!" Let's continue reading.

Verse 26:

Then went the captain with the officers,
and brought them without violence:
for they feared the people,
lest they should have been stoned.

The priest came and grabbed the apostles again! We might as well get ready too because the devil is going to try to mess us up again. We should not be shocked when these things happen. Let's go to Acts 5:38. Here we see one of the council members (Gamiliel) coming forward to speak to the council:

And now I say unto you,
Refrain from these men,
and let them alone:
for if this counsel or this work
be of men, it will come to nought:

Gamiliel told the council that if the work of the apostles was out of the apostles' own spirit, then there was no need to worry. The work would fail. Let's read the next verse.

Verse 39:

But if it be of God, ye cannot
overthrow it; lest haply ye be found
even to fight against God.

He knew that if the apostles' work was of God, it didn't matter if the members of the council jumped, ran, hollered, called "911" or "411!" In other words it didn't matter what the enemy tried to do; God's work would be accomplished and nothing could overthrow it!

Verse 40:

And to him they agreed:
and when they had called the apostles,
and beaten them, they commanded
that they should not speak in
the name of Jesus, and let them go.

The men who were sitting in judgment of the apostles knew people were being saved and delivered. These men had personally witnessed the apostles' deliverance from prison. They agreed that the apostles should be left alone, but they decided to beat them first!

COME OUT OF THE BEATING AND THANK GOD!

We've all seen people who are really anointed. We've seen those who are on fire for God. We've seen people who really know how to get a prayer through and stand in a storm. Believe me, these people have been beaten. They've paid the price to get to that level. There's a price to pay for the anointing. We've paid a price when we learn how to stand through adversity. And when we come out of the beating, thank God that He counted us worthy to suffer this shame (Acts 5:41).

When we really make a stand and commit to the Lord, we're going to be presented with adversity but Jesus comforts us saying:

These things I have spoken unto you,
that in me ye might have peace.
In the world ye shall have tribulation:
but be of good cheer;
I have overcome the world.
(John 16:33)

We may not be physically placed in prison, or physically beaten but the enemy will attack us. And, he may come back to lock us up. If he finds us, we'll still be holding our heads high. We'll still have the joy that comes from the Word of God that says, "I can do all things through Christ which strengtheneth me" (Phil. 4:13). The apostle Peter offers these words of encouragement:

Beloved, think it not strange
concerning the fiery trial
which is to try you,
as though some strange thing
happened unto you:

But rejoice, inasmuch as ye
are partakers of Christ's sufferings;
that, when his glory shall be revealed,
ye may be glad also
with exceeding joy.
(1 Pet. 4:12–13)

CRUCIFYING JESUS AFRESH

If they shall fall away, to renew them again unto repentance; seeing they crucify to themselves the Son of God afresh, and put him to an open shame.
(Heb. 6:6)

When people continue in a lifestyle of *spiritual adultery*, the Bible says it is as if they are crucifying Jesus all over again. They're making His blood sacrifice of non-effect.

Let's ask the Lord, as David did in Psalm 51, to create in us a clean heart. We need to tell the Lord we're sorry and ask Him to forgive our sins. And if the Lord finds any wicked way in us, that He lead us in the way everlasting (Ps. 139:24).

Therefore, my beloved brethen, be ye steadfast, unmoveable, always abounding in the work of the Lord, forasmuch as ye know that your labour is not in vain in the Lord.
(1 Cor. 15:58)

The Lord wants to do exceeding abundantly above all that we ask or think (Eph. 3:20). Our labor is not in vain. All He needs from us is to be committed to Him; to be steadfast and unmoveable, always abounding in the work of the Lord. I can hear the Lord saying, "I'm ready to bless my people. I'm ready to lift them up. I'm ready to take them to a higher place. I'm ready to *release wealth and riches into their lives.*" He's ready to give us *the blessing of commitment.*

TEN

THE LUST FACTOR

The word *holy* exemplifies the character of God. The Greek word for holy is *hagios*, which means to be set apart—sanctified—consecrated. The Bible tells us to be holy for He is holy (1 Pet. 1:16). When we are holy, we are like God and He is glorified.

The enemy, of course, does not want us to live holy—he wants us to sin. He wants us to entertain ideas that are not pleasing to God. Satan wants to get our minds defiled with impure thoughts. Ultimately, the enemy wants to stop our praise because he knows when our praises go up, God's blessings come down.

It is important for us to understand the trickery of the enemy. The devil is shrewd. He doesn't come all at once; he moves in little by little. We cannot allow him to get us out of position and miss the blessings of God. Let's begin in the book of James to see how the deceiver maneuvers to draw us out and knock us down.

But every man is tempted, when he is drawn away of his own lust, and enticed.
(James 1:14)

James is describing what I call *the lust factor*. *Lust*, as it is used in this Scripture, is derived from the Greek word *epithumia*, which means an active and individual desire resulting from *pathos*. Pathos is a state of being "diseased"—to wound, hurt, or suffer. Here pathos is describing the soul's diseased condition. Lust, therefore, is an active desire resulting from a diseased soul.

James tells us that man (or woman) is drawn away from the things of God by his *own* lust, i.e. by the desires of his soul. The devil has done his research. He's not going to tempt you with a box of cigars if he knows you can't stand the smell of them. He knows the things that are enticing to you. He knows which thoughts to plant in your mind. He knows what to do to discourage you from meditating and concentrating on the goodness of God.

No one is exempt from being tempted. Even though you might be saved, your flesh is still vulnerable to temptation. There's something about you the enemy will use to try and inch his way in. Knowing this does not mean that you have an excuse to practice sin—there's never any excuse to sin. What this does mean is that you must stay before God, because in the flesh there is no good thing (Rom. 7:18). Let's study this further.

Then when lust hath conceived, it bringeth forth sin: and sin, when it is finished, bringeth forth death.
(James 1:15)

When lust is conceived or "takes hold" it gives birth to sin; and the end result of sin is death. James is speaking not only of physical death but of spiritual death as well. There are Christians today all over the world who are spiritually dead; unfortunately they don't know it. It is not my desire to buy flowers and grave markers for the spiritually deceased. My desire is for you to know and obey the Word of God so that you can become spiritually resurrected!

Most people don't just jump up and commit sin; they think about it first. Lustful desires get into the mind before someone acts on them. It is not a sin to use our imagination. God loves for us to have an imagination and a vision of doing things to please Him. It is sinful to imagine things that exalt themselves against the knowledge and the will of God. Let's go to 2 Corinthians 10:5:

Casting down imaginations, and every high thing that exalteth itself against the knowledge of God, and bringing into captivity every thought to the obedience of Christ;

The Word of God tells us that every thought, reasoning, or notion we have that contradicts the knowledge of God must be brought into captivity. These imaginations must be captured and made to obey Christ. Remember, Romans 12:2 says that we are transformed by the renewing of our minds. Therefore, as thoughts come to our minds that are contrary to the Word of God, we must immediately rebuke those thoughts and confess the Word. Ephesians 5:19 tells us:

Speaking to yourselves in psalms and hymns and spiritual songs, singing and making melody in your heart to the Lord.

We may not be able to prevent enticing thoughts from entering our minds, but we certainly can stop them from taking hold and bringing forth sin.

PLACE WRONG THOUGHTS UNDER ARREST

None of us are beyond wrong thoughts entering our minds. When the enemy tries to place a wrong thought in your mind tell him, "This thought is under arrest in the Name of Jesus. Satan, I rebuke you out of my mind!"

If you allow wrong thoughts to stay in your mind, the enemy will keep giving you more of them. After awhile, you're pregnant with those wrong thoughts. *Spiritual adultery* is taking place. As I stated before, spiritual adultery is not limited to sexual sins. Spiritual adultery is anything against the will, way, and Word of God.

What makes the enemy want to put wrong thoughts in your mind? He wants to abort the truth that you are trying to birth and raise up. The truth of God cannot coexist with wrong thoughts. If you get pregnant with the wrong thought, you will bring it forth. Then it will be sin and sin brings about death.

KEEP YOUR MIND ON THE PRAISE

Have you ever seen people come to church tired and sleepy? Some churchgoers cannot rest the night before services.

Do you know why this happens? It happens because the enemy knows that if he can distract people this way, they won't hear the Word. He wants to stop them from praising God and getting their deliverance. There have been occasions where I have "deputized" everyone in the audience at Word of Deliverance to lay hands on anyone sitting next to them who is falling asleep. They are instructed to say, "I command you to wake up in the Name of Jesus." Many have seen a miracle happen when their neighbor wakes up!

I'm just kidding about the miracle. However, I cannot emphasize enough the importance of keeping your mind on the praise. We enter the Lord's gates with thanksgiving and into His courts with praise (Ps. 100:4). The devil wants to stop you from getting into the Lord's court. He will bring a pressing problem, concern, or other issues of the flesh to distract you.

When we have our eyes closed, our hands lifted up, or do our little dance; we are really "entering in." Meanwhile, the intruder is trying anything he can to get into our minds. He knows that deliverance is in the praise, and if we praise God, the anointing is stirred up. Everything that is not right will get right!

It concerns me when I see people sitting in church looking as if they are in a daze. It is dangerous not to acknowledge the presence of God. Sometimes I see people staring at the ceiling like they are "too deep" to praise God. In a way they are too much of something. They are too dead—too spiritually dead!

It's difficult for those who know they are not in a proper relationship with God to praise Him as they should. They're scared to shout. They're scared to run because they know that their feet are so heavy, they might trip and fall. Their hands become too heavy to lift up, glorify, and honor God, so they just sit there. What they don't realize is if they made the effort to praise God, His refining fire would stir up again within them.

Some of you do not praise as you should during church services because you're looking around thinking, *Lord have mercy. I don't know why she has that color on; that color just does not look good on her. Lord Jesus, help her! Lord help that brother over there praising God. He's had on the same pants three Sundays in a row. He's had those pants on so long they're shining!*

This is the trickery of the enemy. He plants thoughts to take your mind off what you should be doing. After a while it can become a habit. Before you realize it, you do not have any time left to praise God because you have been so busy checking everyone out. As we enter into the house of the Lord, we must control our thoughts and keep our minds on the praise.

DO A SELF-CHECK

Some Christians believe they should be able to live any way they choose, wear anything they want, and go anywhere they please. They say, "Honey, I'm free. I can wear mini-dresses if I want to because the Holy Ghost made me free!"

You may be able to wear a mini-dress at some churches, but at a church like Word of Deliverance, when the anointing gets stirred up, we raise our hands and praise God. That mini-dress will rise up and make it difficult for the brothers in the church to keep their minds on the praise. Now if the only dress you have is the short one, wear it! But the next time you get paid, as soon as you pay your tithes, go to the store and buy one that comes down to your knees.

Many times when ministers talk about inappropriate attire, they do not deal with the men. But sometimes the men's pants are too tight and their shirts are unbuttoned too far down. The sisters in the church could be shouting. Then they look over and see these men's chest hairs, or see them dressed this way and think, *Glory! He's the one! That's him. I saw him in my dream!*

Casting down imaginations and bringing into captivity your own thoughts is about doing a self-check. On another level, doing a self-check is also about making sure that you are not presenting yourself as a source of temptation to someone else. In both cases, you must check yourself.

JESUS IS OUR PEACE

Peace I leave with you,
my peace I give unto you:
not as the world giveth, give I unto you.
Let not your heart be troubled,
neither let it be afraid.
(John 14:27)

There's a song I like to sing when the enemy is trying to disturb me. It's called *You are My Peace*. Some of you may have cried last night. You may have gone to bed really troubled. Don't wait until the next service at your church to send up praises. Go in your bedroom, your bathroom, your closet, or wherever you need to go and sing, "You are my peace." You'll feel like you have a church full of people right there with you.

I have tried it and know what I am talking about. You really haven't learned how to have "church" until you can do it by yourself. I have been in situations where I have had to praise the Lord all by myself. It didn't matter if no one else was there to praise Him because I know how to get my own "praise on."

The devil tries to disturb you so that you'll have a big pity party. He wants you to feel depressed. He says to himself, *I'm getting ready for the kill. I have her right where I want her. She's crying, she does not have any friends, and nobody understands her. She's lost this and she's lost that.* This is when you need to mess up the devil! Sing to the Lord, "You are my peace, and I worship you."

The devil might not leave right away. He'll try to keep your mind in turmoil. He'll keep on talking. He will tell you, "Honey, that singing will only get you in more trouble. Just hush up and sit down somewhere." This is when you have to stand still and sing, "Peace, Peace."

There's a reason why the enemy doesn't want you to sing praises about the peace of the Lord. He knows this brings in the host of heaven. Psalms 22:3 says:

But thou art holy,
O thou that inhabitest
the praises of Israel.

The Lord lives among the praises of His people. Everyone should know how to sing praises to the Lord. You should sing praises even if you have just awakened and your voice sounds terrible. It really doesn't matter how terrible your voice sounds. Your voice can be raggedy, rugged, messed up and off-key. What God hears is sweet-sounding praises coming from your heart. When you keep praising Him and mean it, He hears you and promises to give you peace. The Scriptures tell us:

Thou wilt keep him in perfect peace,
whose mind is stayed on thee:
because he trusteth in thee.
(Isa. 26:3)

And the peace of God,
which passeth all understanding,
shall keep your hearts and minds
through Christ Jesus.
(Phil. 4:7)

SURRENDER ALL

Your praise shows that you acknowledge who God is. You are reverencing Him when you tell Him, "You are my *Jehovah-shalom*. You are my victory and my peace. I lift my hands not according to what I see, but according to what I believe. I am determined to stay in position whereby I may receive *the blessing of commitment and have wealth and riches released into my life*. I place any thought that exalts itself against You under arrest. I totally commit to Your will, Your way and Your Word. Lord, I lift everything to You right now. I surrender all."

ELEVEN

THE BATTLE IS THE LORD'S

I am a preacher who believes in following the direction and the leading of the Lord. I'm not stuck in a fixed position where God can't tell me, "I need you to do something else." There have been times when I had to make decisions that did not follow the "normal" mode of doing things. One Sunday afternoon, a day before the Labor Day holiday, was one of those times.

The Lord had moved mightily in the morning services as I continued teaching on *the blessing of commitment: releasing wealth and riches into your life.* I had preached on the topic of total spiritual commitment and the need for a spiritual foundation. That afternoon, the Lord allowed me to see a dark cloud attempting to overtake Word of Deliverance. I saw the enemy standing over the congregation. Satan was holding what looked like a big, thick chain. He just stood there, waiting to entangle and bind the saints.

The enemy came to attack during a time when we had been declaring our liberty and victory in God. Yokes were being destroyed. Spirits had been cursed and cast out. We were piercing a higher level of darkness, a place in the spirit realm that the enemy wanted to hold for himself.

"CALL THE SAINTS IN"

After the Lord showed me this, He told me to do something very unusual. He wouldn't allow me to go to dinner or do anything else. He said, "Call the saints in." He instructed me to hold an *emergency prayer revival* for three nights.

This meant calling the congregation in on a holiday. I had never heard of such a thing! Normally, when the spirit leads me to have a revival, an announcement giving the congregation several months notice is sent out. We usually never have less than three weeks notice. "Normal" churches don't call people on a holiday saying, "The Holy Ghost said, 'Prayer tonight'!" But Word of Deliverance is not called to do normal work. Even though it was a holiday, there was work to be done.

We began calling every member that Sunday afternoon. I had ushers calling other ushers, choir members calling other choir members, and greeters calling other greeters. We announced the prayer revival at the Sunday night service. My office staff contacted members not on a committee. Many were called on Labor Day.

I know that I did not get where I am by myself. So when God gives me an instruction, no matter how crazy it sounds,

I'm going to do it. Now, of course I was thinking, *Tomorrow is Labor Day. Everyone is planning on relaxing, barbecuing, and having friends over. How can I tell them to be at church on a holiday?* And I'm sure my church members wanted to tell me, "It's my day off Bishop. I have ribs to eat. What do you mean come pray tonight!" But I didn't let that stop me. I was calling everyone in with every ounce of spirit God had in me. There was an attack being mounted upon the saints of God. We had to come together as one spiritual unit to curse and crush it. We could not allow that demon to wrap his chain around the saints.

SEND US A WORD

Because God was doing something so significant and marvelous, I wanted the congregation to hear from the Lord, especially since I had everyone coming in on a holiday. I asked God to send us a word.

I thought about helping God out: *Maybe I should call someone who will come and deliver a Word from God. They can get on a plane tomorrow and be here Monday night.* But then I said, "God, I'm not going to worry about it. I'm not going to interfere with your business. You do it." I didn't tell anyone about this. It was between the Lord and me.

That Monday while my staff was in the office calling our members, someone called the church and told them, "I have a letter I must give to Bishop Hilton before tonight." My staff told this gentleman where to leave it. When I arrived at the church at 4:30 that afternoon the letter was sticking out of the mailbox. It contained a personal rhema word to Word of Deliverance.

We serve an awesome God. He sent us a *word of knowledge and prophecy* from someone I had never even met! Let me share some of the highlights of that prophetic message with you:

You have been chosen for a very privileged position in these last days. You are being positioned in a most strategic position to storm the very gates of hell for the cause and glory of the Lord Jesus Christ.

...I have selected this church to go far beyond the norm of the average in the realm of worship as the warfare which demolishes principalities and powers in the upper echelons of the heavens. It is a priceless privilege I bestow upon you, My dear children! Your church and pastor are an important part of My master plan to route and destroy the enemy's strongholds in these last days. I will use this church mightily to My glory, if they remain faithful to Me and their lamp does not go out. Hold on tight to Me church. There will surely be difficult days ahead and yet the sheer brilliance of My incomparable glory will outshine and outlast the most ominous and threatening clouds of darkness!

...You, My glorious church, are on the front lines for My kingdom. To present by praise a complete resistance to the enemy forces just as ***Jehoshaphat's Choir Brigade*** *was marching out against a vast multitude of opposition, yet worshipping Me by singing the glad refrain,* ***Praise the Lord for His Mercy Endures Forever.***

...Remain faithful to Me and I will surely counter attack every single move of the enemy against you! Remember Me as the Lion of Judah, which literally means that I manifest Myself as a roaring, conquering Lion when you praise Me—and I devour the enemy.

...You are My ***pride and joy*** *and with Me you will roar against the enemy and conquer in My name and by My anointed presence and power among you! Say,* ***Roar, Lion of Judah, Roar*** *and the devil's brigade will be defeated just by the very breath of My mouth! Have I not promised saying, "Even the captives of the mighty shall be taken away and the prey of the terrible shall be delivered. For I will contend with him that contendeth with thee, and I will save thy children." I, the Lord, have spoken.*

God told us to remain faithful to Him, resist the enemy forces with praise and worship, and He would counterattack every move the enemy made toward us. He also said He would manifest Himself like a roaring, conquering lion and devour the enemy as we praised Him.

AT A MOMENT'S NOTICE

At a moment's notice people came to the church that evening by the hundreds. I knew when the Lord called us in we had to search ourselves. We fell on our knees calling on the Name of Jesus. We cried out, "Lord, help us now. Lord, purify us now." I asked God to move like He had with King Jehoshaphat. Let's look at 2 Chronicles, chapter 20, to see how the enemy was conquered when he tried to come against King Jehoshaphat and his people:

IT came to pass after this also,
that the children of Moab,
and the children of Ammon,
and with them other beside the Ammonites,
came against Jehoshaphat to battle.

Then there came some that told
Jehoshaphat, saying, There cometh
a great multitude against thee
from beyond the sea
on this side Syria; and, behold,
they be in Hazazon-tamar,
which is Engedi.

And Jehoshaphat feared, and set himself
to seek the LORD, and proclaimed
a fast throughout all Judah.
(2 Chron. 20:1–3)

The enemy was planning to attack King Jehoshaphat and the people of Judah. When the king learned about the enemy's plans, they had already entered his territory. This was at a time when King Jehoshaphat had been making great strides in reforming Judah. The people were turning away from worshipping idols and false gods, and renewing their commitment to the God of Abraham, Isaac, and Jacob and His commandments.

Whenever we declare something for the Lord, the enemy is going to come against us. He's going to do his best to get us to take it back. He wants us to hush up, sit down, and not give God perfected praise.

*And Judah gathered themselves together,
to ask help of the LORD; even out of all the
cities of Judah they came to seek the LORD.
(2 Chron. 20:4)*

King Jehoshaphat called all the men, women, and children of Judah together to seek the Lord. In other words, he called an *emergency prayer revival!* King Jehoshaphat knew what to do when his kingdom was in danger of an attack.

*O our God, wilt thou not judge them? for we
have no might against this great company
that cometh against us; neither know we
what to do: but our eyes are upon thee.*

*And all Judah stood before the LORD, with
their little ones, their wives, and their children.
(2 Chron. 20:12–13)*

Let me explain what is happening here. The Word of God says that the weapons of our warfare are not carnal, but they are mighty through God to the pulling down of strongholds (2 Cor. 10:4). During critical times such as these, we cannot be afraid of the devil. Just as the people of Judah stood before the Lord, there was no time for anyone to sit back; the entire congregation at Word of Deliverance called on the Lord.

*Then upon Jahaziel the son of Zechariah,
the son of Benaiah, the son of Jeiel,
the son of Mattaniah, a Levite of the
sons of Asaph, came the Spirit of the LORD
in the midst of the congregation;*

And he said, Hearken ye, all Judah,
and ye inhabitants of Jerusalem,
and thou king Jehoshaphat, Thus saith the
LORD unto you, Be not afraid nor dismayed
by reason of this great multitude;
for the battle is not yours, but God's.

To morrow go ye down against them:
behold, they come up by the cliff of Ziz;
and ye shall find them at the end of the
brook, before the wilderness of Jeruel.

Ye shall not need to fight in this battle:
set yourselves, stand ye still, and see the
salvation of the LORD with you,
O Judah and Jerusalem: fear not,
nor be dismayed; to morrow go out against
them: for the LORD will be with you.
(2 Chron. 20:14–17)

The Spirit of the Lord came upon Jahaziel and he began to speak to the people to let them know that they did not need to fight this battle. Jahaziel told them they didn't have a thing to worry about for *the battle was not theirs, but God's*. He told King Jehoshaphat and Judah to go out on the cliff of Ziz to meet the enemy.

Jahaziel is not mentioned in the Bible before these four verses nor is he mentioned after. But God gave Jahaziel a phenomenal Word to deliver to Jehoshaphat and the people of Judah.

The God we serve is mighty and awesome. He is the same yesterday, today, and forever (Heb. 13:8). Just as He moved upon Jahaziel in the time of King Jehoshaphat, He sent a man I had never met to give a word of knowledge and prophecy to Word of Deliverance. I do not believe any of it happened by coincidence. I believe we were divinely appointed for such a time. God had this ministry, the date, and the hour in His mind before the foundation of the world.

KING JEHOSHAPHAT'S PRAISE TEAM

The Word of God lets us know that King Jehoshaphat put some praisers and singers together, i.e. his *praise team*, and they went out before the enemy and began to send up praises. King Jehoshaphat instructed them to praise the beauty of holiness singing, "Praise the Lord for his mercy endureth forever" (2 Chron. 20:21).

Judah knew how to praise the Lord. When Judah praised God, He would move. God will always remember Judah. He always remembers those who praise Him.

JUDAH

Let's take a few moments to get an understanding of how Judah, whose name in Hebrew means "praise" came about. In Genesis, chapter 29, we see that Judah was the fourth son of Leah and Jacob. Leah was not the woman Jacob really wanted to marry. He really wanted to marry Rachel, Leah's younger sister. Jacob worked for their father, Laban, for seven years to marry Rachel. But on the evening of the wedding feast, Laban *slipped* Leah in. Jacob thought he was sleeping with Rachel, but it was really Leah.

In the morning sunlight, Jacob saw it was Leah who he had been with during the night. He asked Laban, "Why did you do this to me? I worked for Rachel." Laban explained that Rachel was his younger daughter. It would have been against their custom for him to give Jacob his younger daughter before the eldest was betrothed. Since Jacob still wanted Rachel, he had to work an additional seven years to marry her too.

Leah, in an attempt to make Jacob love her, began having sons. The oldest was Reuben [which means, "See, a son!"]. She had another son named Simeon [God hears]. She thought, *Maybe my husband will love me now*. She had another son named Levi [Joining/companion]. But after all of these attempts to make her husband love her, Jacob still did not love Leah as he loved Rachel. When her fourth son was born Leah said, "Now I will praise the Lord. I don't care what Jacob says. I don't care what's happening in this household. I'm just going to praise God. This son shall be named Judah."

Judah became the greatest of all twelve tribes of Israel. Judah was the strongest because Judah stood for praise. God loves praise; He inhabits the praises of His people (Ps. 22:3). He will go to battle for anyone who praises Him.

ROAR, LION OF JUDAH, ROAR

And when they began to sing and to praise, the LORD set ***ambushments*** *against the children of Ammon, Moab, and mount Seir, which were come against Judah; and they were smitten.*

For the children of Ammon and Moab stood up against the inhabitants of Seir, utterly to slay and destroy them: and when they had made an end of the inhabitants of Seir, every one helped to destroy another.
(2 Chron. 20:22)

God said, "When you praise Me, I'm going to be a lion for you and defeat your enemies." The Bible tells us Jesus Christ is the Lion of the tribe of Judah (Rev. 5:5). The lion symbolizes power, authority, majesty and courage.

The lion, even though he is mighty and powerful, destroys his prey by *ambushing* them. He will get in a thicket of bushes and wait for his prey. When the prey comes by, the lion ambushes it by coming out of the bushes and roaring. His roar will cause that prey to do one of two things: the roar will frighten the prey so badly that it will just fall over and the lion will grab it by the neck. Or, it will *run like crazy* trying to get away from the lion.

I don't care which one the devil chooses to do. He can fall over and give up or he can run. Whichever one he does, when the lion roars, the devil is defeated!

THE LORD SET AMBUSHMENTS

At the moment Judah began to sing and send praises, 2 Chronicles 20:22 says that the Lord set ambushments. The Lion of Judah got in the bushes and began to look for the enemy. When He saw the enemy, He roared and attacked them.

The lion's roar was so magnificent that the children of Ammon, Moab, and everyone else with them became confused and began to attack each other. They devoured each other until no one was left (vv. 23–24).

Remember Jahaziel had prophesied that King Jehoshaphat and his people would not have to fight in this battle. In 2 Chronicles 20:17 he said:

Ye shall not need to fight in this battle:
set yourselves, stand ye still, and see the
salvation of the LORD with you,
O Judah and Jerusalem: fear not, nor be
dismayed; to morrow go out against them:
for the LORD will be with you.

In other words, he told them to get in position, stand still, and watch how the Lord would deliver them.

And when Jehoshaphat and his people
came to take away the spoil of them,
they found among them in abundance both
riches with the dead bodies, and precious
jewels, which they stripped off for themselves,
more than they could carry away;
and they were three days in gathering
of the spoil, it was so much.
(2 Chron. 20:25)

By the time King Jehoshaphat and the people of Judah got to the place where the enemy was, the battle was over. They went down to take the spoil. There was such an abundance of *wealth and riches* among the dead bodies that it took them three days to collect all of it!

THE DEVIL IS DEFEATED

The devil is rebuked anytime several hundred people come to church at a moment's notice on a holiday. Cars were lined up and down the street. The community must have been asking, "What is happening at Word of Deliverance?"

God told us if we remained faithful and praised Him, He would manifest Himself as a roaring, conquering lion and defeat the enemy. God did what He said He would do. During the prayer service that Labor Day evening, I saw the cloud move away. It was an awesome experience to see the darkness lifted. We came before God corporately and I believe we were blessed corporately and individually. Hallelujah!

When there is trouble in your home and it looks like things are ready to fall apart, don't start screaming. Start singing a praise song. The Lion of Judah will roar in the midst of your praise. When the difficult times come, simply say, "Roar, Lion of Judah, roar. I'm not going to get upset about this. I'm not going to get worried about this." The Lord remembers those who praise Him and are committed to Him. That trouble is just another opportunity for the Lion of Judah to roar. *The battle is not yours, it's the Lord's.*

TWELVE

RUN WITH PATIENCE

WHEREFORE, seeing we also are
compassed about with so great a cloud
of witnesses, let us lay aside every weight, and
*the sin which so easily beset us, and let us **run***
***with patience** the race that is set before us.*

Looking unto Jesus the author and finisher
of our faith; who for the joy that was set
before him endured the cross,
despising the shame, and is set down
at the right hand of the throne of God.
(Heb. 12:1–2)

Throughout the Bible we find the testimonies of witnesses declaring who God is and what He will do. Abel was a witness. Enoch was a witness. Noah was a witness. Abraham certainly knew how being committed *released wealth and riches into his life!* Moses and the children of Israel crossed the Red Sea on dry ground. When they looked to see where the Egyptians were, they saw their dead bodies on the seashore. These and many more in the Bible were witnesses and had testimonies of what the Lord will do for those who are committed to Him.

Hearing about Jesus is one thing; being a witness and experiencing His saving power is another. Many of us today are witnesses. We know what Jesus has done for us. We know He's a deliverer and a healer. We know Jesus will make things better. He's our Savior and keeper. He's a mind regulator. He's still freeing people from the bondage of the enemy.

Our God is an on-time God. He's a prayer-answering God. He's the Creator, and therefore He's creative. If you need something that can't be found anywhere, He'll create it especially for you. He's a God who *releases wealth and riches into your life!*

Every true believer has a race and a course to run. God has a purpose for your life. To do what God has called you to do and go where He has called you to go, you must be patient. Galatians 6:9 reminds us:

> *And let us not be weary in well doing: for in due season we shall reap, if we faint not.*

Wait on God understanding that He is working out any difficulty you may encounter. You'll have a testimony that God blessed and brought you out.

Let's take a closer look at the words of advice the writer of Hebrews gives to the body of Christ:

...let us lay aside every weight, and the sin which doth so easily beset us, and let us run with patience the race that is set before us. *(Heb. 12:1b)*

Any hindrance that would delay us from running the race and missing the promises of God must be put away. We cannot allow our spirits to be weighted down with sin—it's time to obtain every promise God has for us.

The devil will try to trick us. He'll suggest excuses for us to use, justifying our involvement with his "tools." He wants to knock us off course. But if something was a sin last year, it's still a sin this year. If it's sin, it's just sin, and it is not acceptable before God. So let us lay aside every hindrance and any sin that would stop us from obtaining *the blessing of commitment and God's release of wealth and riches into our lives.*

GOING THROUGH

We often hear the saints talking about "going through." This is a way of saying someone is dealing with a major difficulty or problem. Something is really going wrong and if it's not one thing it's another.

Through is when you have been talked about and scandalized. Your money is gone, your body is hurting, or your children are acting up. Your family is a wreck. When you're going through you don't know how things are going to work out.

The adversary thinks he can defeat us when we are going through. He tells himself, *I can get them now. I can discourage them. I can stop them from singing and raising their hands. I can stop them because they're going through.*

THE OTHER SIDE OF THROUGH

The adversary mounts his biggest attacks against the saints when we are going through. We know from the Word of God that even Jesus endured the cross for the joy that was set before Him (Heb. 1:2). Because He could envision what was on the other side of His through, Jesus could deal with the bitter cup that was set before Him. He knew victory was on the other side.

To hang in there and keep on going in the through times, we need a glimpse and a vision of what's on the other side. We're not running the race because things are going well right now; we run because we understand there's a blessing on the other side of our through.

Let's go to Acts, chapter 16, and see how Paul and Silas made it through. Here we find Paul and Silas having major problems.

Verse 22:

> *And the multitude rose up together against them: and the magistrates rent off their clothes and commanded to beat them.*

A large crowd of people rose up against Paul and Silas. Paul had cast a demon out of a woman who was a fortune-teller.

Many of these people were using this woman's fortune-telling abilities to make money. When Paul cast the demon out, they saw that their money was being cut off. The people were so mad they tore Paul and Silas' clothes off and beat them! Now this is what I call a serious situation. Paul and Silas are going through.

Verse 23:

And when they had laid many stripes upon them, they cast them into prison, charging the jailor to keep them safely:

Many Christians do not think that God would allow them to suffer or get beaten. But, depending on the level of anointing that God has purposed for you to operate in, He may allow you to experience a great deal of pressure. God knows the people who your ministry will touch. He knows the ones you are going to lay hands on. He knows where you will preach and whom you will teach. He doesn't stop your through because He wants your testimony to come from experience. He's a God who loves for us to speak from personal experience. Romans 8:28 assures us:

And we know that all things work together for good to them that love God, to them who are the called according to his purpose.

Paul and Silas took many stripes. I'm sure they wanted to be delivered before they took any stripes; all of us want to be delivered before any stripes come. Yet sometimes, God won't deliver us until after we've experienced some pain.

If anyone is going to quit, it's during times like these. This is when people turn in their resignations. This is when someone tells me, "Pastor, I'm not doing this anymore." People generally quit when they see the stripes coming.

GOD IS STILL GOD

To keep running this race you must understand that God is still God. When you know that He is still God, though you may still get some stripes, you won't let go of your commitment. Let's continue reading Acts, chapter 16. Verse 24–25:

Who, having received such a charge,
thrust them into the inner prison,
and made their feet fast in the stocks.

And at midnight Paul and Silas prayed,
and sang praises unto God:
and the prisoners heard them.

Paul always praised God while he was going through. If you are determined to do work for the Lord, you will need to pray and sing praises during your through time. And you must hold fast to your faith and remember that God is still God.

BE READY

Paul and Silas weren't trying to cause any problems, nor were they trying to bother anyone. They were going about doing the works of Jesus. The trouble started when that woman with the demon started harassing them (Acts 16:16–18).

Knowing the adversary is going to come after us when we do something for God, we must be ready to attack him. When we make a commitment to God, we better be ready to fight. We must have 2 Corinthians 10:4 in our hearts that lets us know our weapons are not carnal, but they are mighty through God. We're wearing our breastplate of righteousness and our shield of faith (Eph. 6:14–15).

The Word says that no weapon formed against us shall prosper (Isa. 54:17). If we read this Scripture carefully, we see that weapons are formed. We should not be shocked when we find weapons formed against us. We should not be surprised when we find ourselves in a through season. Paul and Silas knew what to do in their through. Let's return to Acts, chapter 16, and see what happened to Paul and Silas after they began praising God.

Verse 26:

And suddenly there was a great
earthquake, so that the foundations
of the prison were shaken:
and immediately all the doors
were opened, and every one's
bands were loosed.

If we praise God during the through season, those weapons formed against us will not prosper. They won't grow. Just as God sent an earthquake in Paul and Silas' time to deliver them, He can send one today. We must be ready for spiritual warfare, armed with prayer and praise, knowing there's a miracle on the other side of through.

TRUST GOD

Have you ever seen someone who was going through? Sometimes we can just look at people and know they are depressed, overwhelmed, sick, or burdened. You may have heard about someone in your church that is going through difficult times. Or you yourself may be going through a season of affliction.

When people think someone is going through, they expect that person to have a certain demeanor. Church members may have heard about the problems you are having and therefore expect to see you sitting on the pew looking down. They pity you and anticipate that when they see you, you'll look terrible and have tears in your eyes.

You need to do something that will shock these people and blow their minds! When they expect you to be sitting in a corner looking depressed, get up and dance like you're losing your mind. They'll ask you, "What happened?" You can tell them, "Honey, nothing has changed. I'm just praising God in the through. Not a thing is going on different. I am trusting God!"

ON THE EDGE

The stripes we may have to take while running this race are real. This is not a fairy tale. The God I serve will tell us to do some strange things. The Bible tells us He selects the things in the world that are foolish to put the wise to shame (1 Cor. 1:27). When God gives His people a work to do we must be ready for the adversary because he certainly is going to come after us.

I'm a preacher who the Lord has always sent out on the edge. He has never allowed me to be comfortable. Early in my ministry, I put up a tent on a corner in one of Cincinnati's toughest inner-city neighborhoods. My brother-in-law, Larry Southall, would go with me to pass out tracts in the West End of downtown Cincinnati. (This was our street ministry!)

I wondered why the Lord had me preaching under a tent, while other preachers were in comfortable surroundings. The Lord wouldn't let me go where the people were *asking* for a preacher. He wouldn't let me sit in safety behind the doors of a church building. He had me go out on the streets telling people, "Jesus is coming—get your life in order!" I learned early on that running the race and being committed to God sometimes required operating on the edge.

CHURCH OF DELIVERANCE

Word of Deliverance Ministries for the World, Inc. was birthed from Church of Deliverance; a church started by my father, Lewis Hilton, Sr. At one time my father's church was located in an area of Cincinnati known for its racial intolerance. We didn't mind that because we were there to do the works of Jesus.

One Friday night, in 1981, we were having a revival service. That year stands out in my mind because I had a new Thunderbird and my father had a new Cadillac. During the service, we heard a big bang. While the visiting evangelist was still preaching, the congregation (all fifteen of us!) got up to see what was going on. We told the evangelist to continue preaching—we would be right back!

When I got outside, I looked over at my new Thunderbird and my heart dropped. All of the tires had been slashed. The windshield was busted as well as the rear window. They busted the windshield on my father's Cadillac too, but they really tore up my Thunderbird.

I think they had it out for me, and my Thunderbird. I used to go down to the church and walk around like I was daring someone to come near me. I would park my Thunderbird in front of the church. I must be honest, I wasn't as "saved" as I am now. The Lord has helped me since that time. I was just a little saved back then.

Another incident happened at that location. Early one morning around three o'clock, I received a call from the police. They thought they were calling my father, who was pastor at that time. However, since we have the same name, they called me instead. The police told me there had been a break-in at the church. The speakers had been hauled outside and fish heads were put in front of every entrance. But the enemy's tactics didn't work. Even though we had been attacked again, we never canceled a service, not a single Sunday morning or Wednesday night.

God has taught me many things since then. We must never think that we are going to a higher level in God without going through anything. We pay a price for spiritual elevation and promotion in the Kingdom.

STILL ON THE EDGE

God won't allow the disciples of Word of Deliverance to be comfortable, sit back, come to church, and just "rock and roll." He's still sending us out on the edge. We have to go to the next dimension and I thank God for this.

Recently the Lord instructed me to help a pastor whose church was located in a very rough part of town. Drug dealers were hanging out on the corner in front of his church, so we planned a one-night revival on that corner. I encouraged my congregation to go with me to lift up the Name of Jesus. We wanted the drug dealers and addicts to know that Jesus loved them.

Some people won't go to a church like Word of Deliverance where the pastor tells the congregation to meet on a street corner where people are selling crack cocaine and other illegal drugs. These people look at me like I'm crazy. But I don't care, they have been looking at me like that all my life.

FORGET THE PROGRAM

When you're called to work for God, He will not allow you to stay in a comfort zone. If you study your Bible, you'll see that God called some people to do some very unusual things. Let's take Noah for example. When God told Noah to build the ark, it had never rained on the earth. It didn't make sense for a man to build a boat on land, getting ready for something that had never happened before. The people told Noah, "We don't know anything about a flood and we're not getting on that ark."

Sometimes we have to forget "the program." Too many Christians want to stick to a predetermined format and stay within the four walls of the church. Now is the time to go beyond our comfort zone and reach out to those who are lost and in bondage. The real program is about souls getting saved and being delivered.

THE DEVIL'S NO COMPETITION

There is no competition between Jesus and the devil. Satan is not as powerful as he presents himself. The devil is a defeated foe and we must never allow him to stop us from doing the fantastic things God has called us to do.

The enemy is not on our left side while Jesus is on our right, as if they are equal in power. They are *not* equal in power. Matthew 28:18b lets us know that all power is given unto Jesus in Heaven and earth. God created the devil. We need to tell him, "The same God that made you made me. And the same God that is protecting me will check you. You're trespassing on God's property!"

ANOINTED BOUNCE

Any time the enemy is allowed to knock us down, God will put an anointed bounce in our spirits. We'll bounce so high that we end up higher than we were when we started. We don't have to worry when we have trials and tribulations because Jesus said:

These things I have spoken unto you,
that in me ye might have peace.
In the world ye shall have tribulation: but be
of good cheer; I have overcome the world.
(John 16:33)

When you experience tribulation, know that God is just lifting you higher. You're coming up again and you'll be higher than you've ever been.

Many Christians think they are ready for spiritual promotion. But I must warn those who have this desire: you will go through some sufferings. Whenever I see someone whose life gives God glory, I know I'm looking at someone who has endured some adversity. In 2 Corinthians 4:8–9 Paul says:

We are troubled on every side,
yet not distressed; we are perplexed,
but not in despair;

Persecuted, but not forsaken;
cast down, but not destroyed.

In Romans 8:18 Paul also lets us know:

...that the sufferings of this present time
are not worthy to be compared to
the glory which shall be revealed in us.

GET READY! GET SET! GO!

We must count it all joy when we fall into divers temptations (James 1:2). When the storms and the battles of life come, get excited with an expectation of deliverance.

We saw in Proverbs 23:18 that there is surely an end and our expectation shall not be cut off. God just wants to show us His character. We're learning to endure hardness as a good soldier (2 Tim. 2:3). He's setting us up for another testimony.

When the devil comes after us, he can't do anything but take us higher because we're committed and we won't quit. It's just another opportunity for God's glory to be revealed in our lives. Our eyes are on Jesus: He's our example. He's the originator, orchestrator, and developer of our faith. *We're running the race that is set before us with patience.* Get ready! Get set! Go...

THIRTEEN

COMMIT TO A HOLY LIFE

People ask me on many occasions, "What is the real evidence that a person has received the baptism of the Holy Spirit? What is the real proof that He lives inside of someone? What really determines if God's Spirit is there?" I tell them the real proof is a person's lifestyle. The evidence of whether someone is filled with the Holy Spirit or not can be seen in how they live.

Some Christians believe that speaking in tongues is the evidence of the indwelling of the Holy Spirit. However, I have seen too many "devils" speak in tongues. I have seen "tongue-talkers" committing adultery, fornicating, lying, and cheating. I've seen them skipping, sliding, even peeping, and hiding. Please do not misunderstand me; I am not saying that speaking in tongues is not important. In Jude 20 it says that we are to build ourselves on our most holy faith, praying in the Holy Ghost. But the Word of God also says that those who have become part of God's family do not make a practice of sinning (see 1 John 5:18). The real proof is your life.

WHAT EVIDENCE DOES YOUR LIFE SHOW?

Is your life showing evidence that the Holy Spirit lives in you? A person who is living for God has a certain lifestyle. The Bible says that you know a tree by the fruit it bears. If we are connected to the True Vine, we will bear the fruit of the Spirit which is love, joy, peace, longsuffering, gentleness, goodness, faith, meekness, and temperance (see John 15:1–5 and Gal. 5:22–23).

Unfortunately, many Christians believe they can do whatever they want. We live among the "do what you want" generation. However, when you are living for God you cannot do what you want and remain connected to the True Vine. You must live according to His principles and have your foundation built upon His Word. Without a firm foundation you can easily become double-minded and get confused about how you should be living. Keep your foot on the solid foundation of God's Word so you can receive *the blessing of commitment and a release of wealth and riches into your life!*

HOLINESS IS STILL GOD'S STANDARD

We must continually search ourselves because there is a standard we must live by if we want to be with Christ. Everyday you need to ask yourself if your life is giving God glory. Holiness is still God's standard. Thoughts of envy and strife directed towards you by someone will not hinder you. On the other hand, your thoughts of envy and strife will keep you from seeing Jesus. The lies someone told does not matter; what matters is the lie you told. Your actions, not someone else's, will keep you from obtaining eternal life.

Jesus is coming back for people who have made themselves ready. He is not coming back for people who are contemplating getting ready. He's coming for the ones who *are* ready. We must be ready to meet the soon-coming King!

THEY SHALL BE MINE

The Word of God does not have to be watered-down for people to meet His requirements. God's standard does not have to be lowered because He will always have a remnant of believers who will obey Him. God has people who want to live for Him. We are precious in His sight and belong to Him. As a matter of fact, the Lord said, "And they shall be mine…in that day when I make up my jewels" (Mal. 3:17).

DO THE RIGHT THING

People living in sin should be nervous in the house of God. Sinners should feel uncomfortable sitting in the sanctuary. These churchgoers should be shaking in their boots, fearing that the Holy Ghost will expose them at any moment! Remember the Word of God that says, "…and be sure your sin will find you out" (Num. 32:23b).

An intimate relationship with the Lord requires reading His Word daily and obeying His instructions. If you are finding it difficult to live holy, make a stronger commitment.

When you really get to know who Jesus is, you can maintain a lifestyle of holiness. Anytime the tempter comes you will have a Word of God in you, encouraging you to *do the right thing.*

IT'S NO SECRET

Let's go to the book of Luke. If you want to receive *the blessing of commitment,* you must make sure your life is measuring up to what God requires. Luke 12:2–3 reads:

For there is nothing covered,
that shall not be revealed;
neither hid, that shall not be known.

Therefore whatsoever ye have spoken
in darkness shall be heard in the light;
and that which ye have spoken
in the ear in closets shall be
proclaimed upon the housetops.

Secrets never remain secret. This passage of Scripture tells us that everything done in darkness shall be revealed. Your secret is no longer a secret. Remember, the eyes of the Lord are in every place, beholding the evil and the good (Prov. 15:3).

Years ago the older saints would tell us, "Make sure your life is one whereby you may see Jesus face to face." I might add, "If you're not going to live holy you might as well get a first class ticket to hell. Why go coach?" Amen.

I delight in obeying the instructions and commandments of the Lord. I am on my way to see Jesus and enjoying the trip. Yet I never forget to stay alert to the enemy's tricks, because the devil will try to tell us how, when, and with whom to sin. We must have so much of the Word of God in us that when the tempter brings to our minds sinful thoughts, the fire of the Holy Ghost burns them up.

RIGHT THINKERS

We must be careful of what we exercise in our minds because God knows all of our thoughts. Ezekiel 11:5 says:

And the Spirit of the Lord fell upon me, and said unto me, Speak; Thus saith the Lord; Thus have ye said, O house of Israel: for I know the things that come into your mind, every one of them.

It is time to be a "right thinker." We must allow God to renew our minds and purge our thoughts according to His Word. When the devil came to tempt Jesus, he brought enticing thoughts to draw Jesus away from the Father's divine plan. The enemy even manipulated Scripture as he tried to convince Jesus to bow down and worship him (see Luke 4:1–3). Just as Jesus had a Word to stand against satan, *right thinkers* must know God's Word. The Bible tells us to cast down every thought that is contrary to the Word of God (2 Cor. 10:4). We must be *right thinkers* and bring every thought in subjection to Christ.

PARENTS MUST SET THE STANDARD

My parents taught me about holiness at a young age. They got saved when I was five years old, so I practically grew up in the church. Our family was in church so often that sometimes the pews were our beds. My parents never asked me if I wanted to go to church, not once. Some children have parents who give them a choice about attending church, but not mine. Even during my teenage years my parents never asked me if I had other plans. I might have intended on hanging out with my friends, but my plans meant nothing to my parents because I was going to church!

On certain days and times, my siblings and I knew where we would be. We would pile into the family car and head for church. Today many families have big vehicles with plenty of room, but the eight of us had to squeeze into a six-passenger car. We would get in the best way we could because no matter what, we all were going to church. On top of that, my parents would pick up people they knew needed transportation. They never hesitated to offer a ride to anyone who needed it.

When my siblings and I reached an age where we began to understand the Word, our parents required a higher level of conduct from us. They set a standard for us to live by and did not allow us to do anything that did not meet their approval. Some of you may not have been raised like this, but I had the kind of parents who were in their children's "business." They would even tell my siblings and me (if we didn't already know), what style of dress and haircut we could wear.

I am going to be honest with you. While growing up I felt my parents were too strict and I did not like it, but my upbringing helped me develop strong morals and values. Their rules and regulations were instilled in me so deeply that I would be too nervous to go anywhere or do anything that went against their standards.

Today there are children who think their parents should not restrict them in any way. But my parents let us know that as long as we were in their house, we had to abide by their rules. Young parents sometimes give their children more freedom than they really need. If you give children too much freedom, they can get hurt. The discipline I received from my parents helped me become the person I am today, and I am glad they raised me the way they did.

LISTEN TO THE MATURE SAINTS

The church benefits from the instruction of mature saints. Some people are getting saved one day and prophesying the next. Those new to a life of holiness must be willing to receive instruction and correction from more experienced believers. Otherwise, they might tell someone who is trying to correct and show them their error that, "God told me to do it!"

Babes in Christ often are not in tune with the voice of God. It takes a lot of experience to discern His voice. Titus, chapter 2, tells us that the aged men and women are to teach the young men and women sound doctrine. Young Christians who lack knowledge should look to the more experienced Christians to help them learn how to live according to God's Word.

I grew up during a time when the mothers in the church could tell a child to "straighten up" and they did not have to worry about the child's parents getting angry. Church mothers could tell someone's daughter that her dress was too short or someone's son that his pants were too tight, without worrying about being confronted by the parents. Unfortunately this does not happen as often today because so many people are easily offended.

The respect and honor older saints received in the church years ago is now hard to find. I encourage the older mothers at Word of Deliverance to develop a relationship with the young ladies. We teach the young ladies to listen to those who can help them so they will know how to stay out of trouble. I also encourage the older men to build relationships with the younger ones. I impress upon the young men to seek guidance from the older men. It does not matter if these men grew up in the 1920's or 40's and it is now a new millennium; the older men can still teach the young men about life.

It is a terrible thing to reject instruction. Proverbs, chapter 1, encourages young men and women to be receptive to the instructions and counsel of those who have attained a higher level of wisdom and understanding. It reads:

The proverbs of Solomon
the son of David, king of Israel;

To know wisdom and instruction;
to perceive the words of understanding;

To receive the instruction of wisdom,
justice, and judgment, and equity;

To give subtlety to the simple, to the young man knowledge and discretion.

A wise man will hear, and will increase learning; and a man of understanding shall attain unto wise counsels;

To understand a proverb, and the interpretation; the words of the wise, and their dark sayings.

The fear of the Lord is the beginning of knowledge; but fools despise wisdom and instruction.

My son, hear the instruction of thy father, and forsake not the law of thy mother:

For they shall be an ornament of grace unto thy head, ...
(Prov. 1:1–9)

Even if you do not understand an instruction that has been given to you, don't reject it. Pray about it, be quiet, and be receptive to the wise counsel of mature saints.

The real proof of the indwelling of the Holy Spirit can be seen in a person's lifestyle. A spirit-filled person delights in following God's instructions, obeying His commands, and living in a manner that pleases Him. God's Spirit gives you power to *commit to a holy life* so you can get in position to receive *the blessing of commitment. Wealth and riches will be released into your life* and the world will know without a doubt that you are blessed!

FOURTEEN

HE LOVES YOU

I thank God for the blessing He has declared over the lives of the saints who are committed to Him. The Lord rewards His children who carefully and diligently seek Him (Heb. 11:6). He wants *wealth and riches released into your life!* Luke 12:32 tells us:

> *Fear not, little flock; for it is your Father's good pleasure to give you the kingdom.*

God is moving us into wonderful and strategic areas. Though you may be going through a storm or battle, be encouraged. God loves His children so much that no weapon the enemy forms against us will be able to prosper (Isa. 54:17). You don't have to worry, cry, or be depressed about anything because *He loves you.* You will not be defeated, destroyed, nor fail because *He loves you!*

I can say this because of the confidence I have in God. There was a time when I would wobble and stumble, but I have learned how to hold fast to God's Word. Going through trials, tribulations, and very difficult times showed me more about His saving grace. The Bible lets us know that the Lord will deliver us out of all our persecutions (2 Tim. 3:11). The troubles I have gone through helped me develop the strength to endure and now I know from personal experience that the Lord will see me through.

GRACE

Grace is the kindness and love of God towards mankind. It is His unmerited favor: we did nothing to earn or deserve it. God's grace gives us the ability to be holy and power to live in a manner that pleases, honors, and glorifies Him. The grace of God lovingly and patiently bears our inadequacies as we learn how to live according to His Word.

Don't be foolish and allow the enemy to trick you and never forget that the devil knows the Word of God too. The adversary will try to convince you that God loves and favors you so much that He will ignore your sin. Satan will tell you, "Go ahead and sin; God understands your weaknesses. After all, He did say that His grace is sufficient."

God's grace really *is* sufficient (2 Cor. 12:9), but the Word of God also says:

What shall we say then? Shall we continue in sin, that grace may abound?

God forbid. ...
(Rom. 6:1–2)

The grace of God should never be used as an escape clause to continue in sin. If someone chooses to reject the Word of God and practice sin, it won't be because I didn't tell that person the truth. I refuse to allow the blood to be required in my hand. Even though *He loves you*, the wages of sin is still death (Rom. 6:23).

WORSHIP HIM

There's something about love. Love will protect and embrace you. It will chastise and spank you. My life has changed since I truly received the Word that because He loves me, the battle is not mine, but God's.

I will always worship God for who He is and what He will do. I realize that no matter what is going on in my life, I can find rest and comfort in His love. He will turn darkness into light and make crooked ways straight. He will create a miracle that is uniquely designed for you. God will place people in your path who are for you and remove those who are against you. He'll open some doors and close others. He's an awesome God worthy of all praise.

Living for God will change your life. He promises to give you *the blessing of commitment and release wealth and riches into your life*, but you must be totally committed to Him. *He loves you* and desires above all things that you prosper and be in health, even as your soul prospers (3 John 2). What a mighty God we serve! Let us adore, love, worship, and thank Him for all He has done for us.

PRAYER OF THANKSGIVING

Father, in the precious Name of Jesus, we thank You for Your grace and mercy. We thank You for saving us from the penalty of sin. Thank You for patiently teaching us by Your Spirit and through Your Word how to be Your people. We thank You for the *blessing of commitment* that declares we are the head, and not the tail and places us above only, and not beneath. We thank You for such a time as this where Your Glory is revealed through us and for the *wealth and riches* You are *releasing* into our lives. Thank You for blessing us so that we may be a blessing. In Jesus' Name. Amen.

PRAYER OF SALVATION

If you don't know Jesus as your personal Lord AND Savior first you must...

KNOW THAT GOD LOVES YOU

"God demonstrates His own love towards us, in that while we were still sinners, Christ died for us." (Romans 5:8 NKJ)

CONFESS YOUR BELIEF IN JESUS

"...that if you confess with your mouth the Lord Jesus and believe in your heart that God has raised Him from the dead, you will be saved." (Romans 10:9 NKJ)

REPENT AND TURN FROM SIN

"Repent therefore and be converted, that your sins may be blotted out..." (Acts 3:19 NKJ)

RECEIVE JESUS CHRIST

"But as many as received Him, to them He gave the right to become children of God, to those who believe in His name." (John 1:12 NKJ)

Then, pray this prayer from your heart:

Jesus, I believe You died for me and that You rose again on the third day. I confess to You that I am a sinner and I need Your love and forgiveness. Come into my life, forgive my sins, and give me eternal life. I confess You now as my Lord and Savior. Thank YOU for my salvation.

COVENANT PARTNERSHIP

Invitation

With all the hurting people in the world today (physically, emotionally and spiritually), God is proving that He is still God all by Himself!

Thousands of people around the world are being ushered into the Kingdom of God on a daily basis. God has given THIS ministry a mandate to ***"Take the Word to the World,"*** and we are accomplishing this with supporters like **YOU**. Our television broadcast is televised nationally on the **Inspiration Network (INSP)** which can also be viewed via internet (www.insp.com)**, The Dream Network, Cable Access Channels** in Ohio and Kentucky, and we are airing live on **1480 WCIN**, a local radio station which can also be heard via internet at (www.1480wcin.com), on Sunday evenings from 8:00 – 9:00 PM.

Several national television networks and radio stations are inviting us to join them, but due to limited funds, we are unable to accept these invitations at this time.

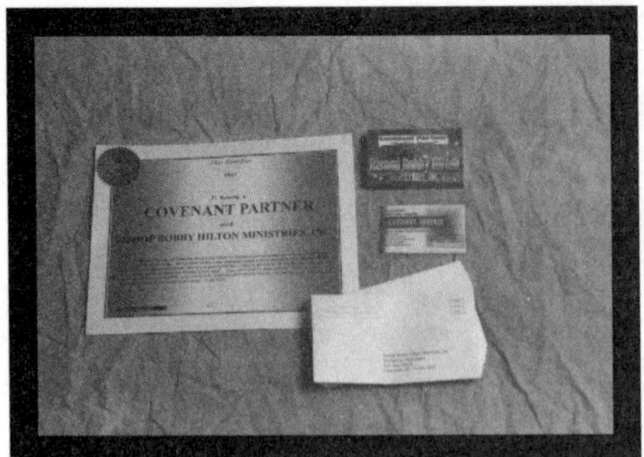

Would you prayerfully consider becoming a PARTNER? If the Lord is touching your heart, please have enough faith and courage to say **"Yes"** to His leading. Join us as a *"Covenant Partner"* today! Your initial Covenant Partner packet will include a FREE audio tape, certificate, and a discount card.

To become a Covenant partner, please write or call us:

Bishop Bobby Hilton Ministries, Inc.
P.O. Box 46545 * Cincinnati, OH 45246
TOLL FREE: 1-877-851-WORD(9673)

Releasing Wealth & Riches Into YOUR Life!

There is a divine blessing over the lives of believers who totally commit to God. Scripture declares that if we follow His instructions and live according to His Word, God will release wealth and riches into our lives (Ps. 112:1–3). In this powerful study, Bishop Bobby Hilton shows you by the Word of God that once you make this commitment, you will not be second place in anything.

The Blessing of Commitment will teach you what it takes to prosper and have victory through Christ Jesus, in every area of your life. God's glory shall be revealed and the world will know that you are blessed!

ITEM#1BK01 - $12.99

To order a copy of this book, please complete the attached Product Order Form and mail to:

Bishop Bobby Hilton Ministries, Inc.
P.O. Box 46545
Cincinnati, OH 45246

To order by phone, please call us toll free:

1-877-851-WORD(9673)

Abiding Under The Shadow

This captivating series will motivate you in your spiritual walk to obtain everything God has declared for your life. You will come to understand that it's not enough just to be a believer, but you must be in proper position to receive spiritual blessings from God. The enemy will try and move you out of position, but through this Word you will become steadfast and unmovable against the wiles of the devil!

(4 Audios) Item# 4T10 $18
(2 Videos) Item# 2VT10 $25

Faith Zone

Learn to develop and increase your sixth sense of "Faith." In "The Faith Zone" you can expect the impossible, see the invisible, feel the intangible and taste the goodness of God! "The Faith Zone" is a spiritual place within where you abide in God and not rely on what you feel, know or think. It is a place where you can be totally dependent on God as He manifests His Word into your life.

(4 Audios) Item# 4T03 $18

Divine Promises

Learn how to receive what belongs to you, as Bishop Bobby Hilton teaches the Word concerning "Divine Promises." In this series you will learn that "Divine Promises" are obtained by holding fast to your profession of faith in Christ Jesus. Circumstances in your life may seem to be encircling you. However, don't be locked in by situations rather than released by what God promised. His "Divine Promises" are still yours!

(4 Audios) Item# 4T15 $18

AUDIO & VIDEO TAPE RESOURCES

Spiritual Things

As you listen to these powerful teachings by Bishop Hilton, you will learn how to grow spiritually mature in God and understand that through your untiring trust in His Word you will become who He has already predestined you to be. You will also begin to understand the importance of a spiritual connection with God and about the 3-dimensions of praise.

(4 Audios) Item# 4T09 $18
(2 Videos) Item# 2VT09 $25

Effectual Fervent Prayer

In this tape series, Bishop Hilton teaches us how to be Effectual Fervent Prayer warriors communicating with God through our praise and worship, and the petitions we place before Him. An Effectual Fervent Prayer warrior is a spiritually well-built person who can endure test, resist temptation and be totally submitted to God.

(4 Audios) Item# 4T13 $18
(2 Videos) Item# 2V13 $25

Anointed

Everyone in the body of Christ has work to do in the ministry. However, it's not good enough to be talented, gifted or skilled. To accomplish the spiritual task set before us, we must be Anointed! It is important to correlate the difference between being graced and being anointed, grace takes you through it, but the anointing take you to it.

(4 Audios) Item# 4T12 $18
(2 Videos) Item# 2VT12 $25

CALL TOLL FREE! (877) 851-WORD(9673)

Bishop Bobby Hilton Ministries, Inc.

PRODUCT ORDER FORM

Name:____

Address:____

City:_______________________________State:______ Zip Code:_________

Telephone: (______)____

METHOD OF PAYMENT: (__) CHECK (__) CHARGE: __VISA __MC __AMEX

CREDIT CARD#: _________/_________/_________/_________ EXP. DATE:_____/_____

Signature:____

Please make all checks payable to: BBHM (Bishop Bobby Hilton Ministries, Inc.)

QTY.	ITEM#	TITLE	PRICE	TOTAL
			SUBTOTAL	
			SHIPPING & HANDLING	
			Ohio Residents Add 6% Tax	
			TOTAL	

SHIPPING & HANDLING RATES

Order Total	*Shipping & Handling*
Up to $5.99	$1.00
$6.00-$15.00	$2.50
$15.00+	$3.50

For mail-in orders, please complete the order form and send along with your payment to:

Bishop Bobby Hilton Ministries, Inc.
P.O. 46545
Cincinnati, OH 45246-0545

TO PLACE YOUR ORDER BY PHONE, CALL US TOLL FREE

(877) 851-WORD(9673)